Praise for
Understanding and Combating Racism:
My Path from Oblivious American to Evolving Activist

"Bill Wynne makes a sincere and wide-ranging examination of his developing consciousness of racism in the US, and he spares neither himself, the Catholic Church, nor the white population in his conclusions, even as he sees hope for the future."

— Kathleen Brady, author of the biographies *Lucille, The Life of Lucille Ball; Francis and Clare: The Struggles of the Saints of Assisi;* and *Ida Tarbell: Portrait of a Muckraker.*

"Bill Wynne's memoir clearly has an agenda: gently yanking me out of my oblivion. By telling his own story, he focused me on important questions of injustice."

— Denis Joseph Stemmle, author of *Puddles from a Drooling Mind, Pope Nobody the Great,* and *Matthew's Dilemma.*

"I've been fortunate to be a witness to the journey Bill Wynne has chronicled here. In fact, his continual push to learn more, understand better, and most importantly to *act* as an anti-racist has often inspired me in my own journey to deeper understanding and action."

— Frank Staropoli, Co-Founder, Exploring Racism Groups

"Few are as dedicated to confronting the lingering impact of racism head-on as Bill is. This book shows his unflinching willingness to examine his own journey as a white American male growing up in the second half of the 20th century and his dedication to forging a path to social and racial justice."

— Paul L. Caccamise, LMSW, ACSW

"This memoir is a lived testimony that is timely and will serve as an example for each of us, especially white males, to be introspective as it relates to race and racism. Reading this with my head and heart gives me hope for the future."
— Gaynelle Wethers, Retired Educator and long-time friend

"Anyone who reads his book with an open mind and an equally open heart will be inspired to examine his/her/their own beliefs and behaviors. Wynne shares his journey with honesty and humility."
— Jane Sutter Brandt, Writer and Editor at Sutter Communications

"Bill Wynne's authentic and engaging narrative melds memoir with social justice and spiritual self-discovery. A thoughtful and inspiring self-inquiry about how we can learn to value the 'other.'"
— Jennifer Leonard,
President & CEO, Rochester Area Community Foundation

"Whether there is agreement or not with the premise set forth in this book, there is no denying Mr. Wynne writes with honesty, insight and conviction. His openness and soul searching makes this book well worth reading."
— Kathleen Petronio, friend and a history advocate by education

"Bill has been a leader in our community for decades, but he wasn't satisfied with the comfort that afforded him. He dares to dig deep into his own life and experiences to provide fresh perspectives on white privilege."
— Scott Benjamin, CEO of Charles Settlement House and The
Community Place of Greater Rochester, N.Y.

"Bill was the first friend to model for me — white guy to white guy — a process for learning how to be anti-racist. I am eternally grateful for how Bill's example has helped me slowly open my heart and mind to the realities of racism and reinforced the message that the hard and difficult 'truth will set you free.'"
— Claude Adair, friend

"More than possibly, we know individuals like Bill Wynne who have opened their life to wonder about what has been going on that their lives seem to be closed; possibly closed in around race or those other things that originally were inconclusive, but as we have opened our eyes, we realize were excluding others and, in fact, painfully dividing a nation that now feels its own division, brokenness and need for healing. Bill's book goes about opening up his story, his movement in that healing that, as it happens within, moves us out to others. Not in some way in which Bill has gone on a campaign, but rather on a conversion, a path of deep inner healing or metanoia, as he notes, a change of heart and mind and because of that, disposition, attitude and the way in which we would work or interact with others."
— Fr. Daniel Riley OFM, Mt. Irenaeus Franciscan Mountain
Community

"The story of Bill's courageous and uncommon journey provides illumination and lessons for us all in understanding and overcoming the challenges to ourselves, our families, our communities and beyond in desiring and working for justice for all people regardless of racial classifications, economics or social status."
— J. Toyer, Contributor, *The Road to Independence: 101 Women's Journeys to Starting Their Own Law Firms.*

"Bill Wynne's journey of self-discovery is as if he is lifting a boiling caldron in his arms and refusing to let go. The scars will run deep and be painful, but Bill's willingness to embrace the moral calling of our time, perhaps of the ages, will make him a better man and a better Christian, perhaps more importantly a better witness to truth. This isn't just a journey for Bill Wynne, it is an imperative for us all."
— Douglas E. Parker, Financial Advisor

Understanding and Combating Racism

My Path from Oblivious American to Evolving Activist

Understanding and Combating Racism

My Path from Oblivious American to Evolving Activist

By W.E. Wynne

PathBinder
Publishing
COLUMBUS,
INDIANA

Published by PathBinder Publishing
P.O. Box 2611
Columbus, IN 47202
www.PathBinderPublishing.com

Copyright © 2021 by W.E. Wynne
All rights reserved

Edited by Krista Hill and Doug Showalter

First published in 2021

Manufactured in the United States

ISBN: 978-1-955088-11-4
Library of Congress Control Number: 2021921341

*To Sandy, who has been tirelessly by my side all these
years and an inspiration to all those she meets
and
Our children, Allyson, Sean, and Andrew for their devotion
and
Our future hope, Jack, Hudson, Ava, Harper ... and all of
their generation.*

Foreword

The subject of race and the issue of racism are in the forefront of all news media today. To say the least, discussions surrounding them are highly charged and emotional. Many different approaches and starting points have been tried. The challenge with even having the discussion is that there is often blaming of the "other," ignorance of the "other," feelings of guilt and shame, or trying to maintain power in many overt and subtle ways.

To quote from Rochester, New York's First Community Interfaith Institute's June/July 2021 newsletter referencing the passing of its founder, National Minister Lawrance Lee Evans Sr.:

> He and others did not waste their time talking about past conditions and situations that currently are not meaningful nor correct. They asked us (Blacks) not to shame or blame white people about what their grandfathers and great grandmothers had done to Blacks. Also, he asked Blacks not to shame the Africans who had the trading posts, sometimes called factories; African chiefs supplied the slaves and sold them to the Europeans, but not only the Europeans but people all over the continent. The African chiefs, Europeans, and others called it blood money and black gold.

Equally, white people are guilty of blaming the "other" (defined as anyone not like "me") for the numerous societal ills we are burdened with today.

I like the above quote since it implies that perhaps there can be a new starting point for conversations. What has troubled me over the years is how so often the Black community, which in so many ways has been oppressed, is also asked to educate the white community on what it's like to be Black.

Bill Wynne gives us a new starting point, not to inflict guilt, but to help the white community and individuals reflect on what it is like to be white. He provides us the opportunity to sort out the many influences (many so subtle that we are quite unaware) that shape how we think, act, and feel about the "other."

Sociologists tell us there are five major influencers in our lives: family, education, economics, religion, and politics. I would add to this list: race, ethnicity, culture, gender, sexual orientation, profession, class, whether we grew up in the city, suburbs, or in a rural area, and intergenerational differences.

Is it any wonder why we have difficulty understanding the "other" when we have never seriously considered what makes us "us" and me "me?"

Bill Wynne has gone through many years of reflection doing just that and his book gives us the permission to do the same. I encourage you, especially white souls, to read it with an open mind and heart.

I close with the following quote from *To Bless the Space Between Us* by John O'Donohue: "Yet later in life, when one might look more closely, it is quite incredible how so many of the roots of one's identity, experience, and presence lead back to that childhood kitchen where so much was happening that was unknown to itself." He continues: "Home is where the heart is. It stands for the sure center where individual life is shaped and from where it journeys forth."

God bless each of your own journeys toward a richer and deeper understanding of yourself and the "others" in your midst.

— Rev. Robert (Bob) Werth
A priest in the Diocese of Rochester since 1979. Nearly his entire career has been spent experiencing the gifts of cultures not his own; first, Black; then, Portuguese; and currently, Latinx. He serves as parochial vicar at St. Frances Xavier Cabrini parish as well as being sacramental minister at Nazareth Elementary School in Rochester, N.Y. He was a social worker for five years before studying for the priesthood.

Preface

In November 2020, Richard Rohr, an American author, spiritual writer, and Franciscan friar based in Albuquerque, New Mexico, wrote about a call for racial justice made decades earlier by Thomas Merton, an American Trappist monk, writer, theologian, mystic, poet, social activist, and scholar of comparative religion. Rohr wrote:

> Amidst the intense struggle for civil rights, Thomas Merton insisted Christians had a moral duty to address racism — on a personal and systemic level. His words were prophetic at the time and continue to be relevant to this day. In *Seeds of Destruction* (1964, the heart of the Civil Rights era), he writes:
>
> "The race question cannot be settled without a profound change of heart, a real shake-up and deep reaching metanoia [Greek for repentance or change of mind] on the part of White [sic] America. It is not just [a] question of a little more good will and generosity: it is a question of waking up to crying injustices and deep-seated problems which are ingrained in the present setup and which, instead of getting better, are going to get worse.
>
> "The purpose of non-violent protest, in its deepest and most spiritual dimensions is then to awaken the conscience of the white people to the awful reality of their injustice and of their sin, so that they will be able to see that the Negro problem is really a White [sic] problem: that the cancer of injustice and hate which is eating white society and is only partly manifested in racial segregation with all its consequences, is rooted in the heart of the white people themselves."

In later writings, Merton elaborates on the pernicious evil of systems of oppression and how we must combat them through faith, hope, and love.

"When a system can, without resort to overt force, compel people to live in conditions of abjection, helplessness, wretchedness ... it is plainly violent. To make people live on a subhuman level against their will, to constrain them in such a way that they have no hope of escaping their condition, is an unjust exercise of force. Those who in some way or other concur in the oppression — and perhaps profit by it — are exercising violence even though they may be preaching pacifism. And their supposedly peaceful laws, which maintain this spurious kind of order, are in fact instruments of violence and oppression.

"Growth, survival and even salvation may depend on the ability to sacrifice what is fictitious and unauthentic in the construction of one's moral, religious or national identity. One must then enter upon a different creative task of reconstruction and renewal. This task can be carried out only in the climate of faith, of hope and of love: these three must be present in some form, even if they amount only to a natural belief in the validity and significance of human choice, a decision to invest human life with some shadow of meaning, a willingness to treat other people as other selves."

***

With the initial draft of my first book drawing to a close, I took a walk on a snowy, late February day. I was blinded by the dazzling white landscape, and it was a challenge to stay on what I thought was the correct path. I began to recall memories of cross-country skiing in the Adirondacks many years ago. Frost's "Stopping by Woods on a Snowy Evening," memorized during my school days, echoed through my mind: "... and miles to go before I sleep."

I was just starting my walk through the woods, with some miles ahead of me, and it struck me that my surroundings provided several metaphors for this memoir. The virgin white carpet of fluffy snow made me think of the blanket of whiteness that had shrouded me throughout my life, providing comfort and protection — namely, the color of my skin. The challenge of staying on the path brought to mind that it would have been nice to have had some contrast and diversity to help guide my way.

Most everything around me was white, making my surroundings monotonous and, to some degree, dangerous. Whether walking in the snow or on life's path, there is a definite need for contrast, which Merriam-Webster defines as any of the following:

• The juxtaposition of dissimilar elements (such as color, tone, or emotion) in a work of art.

• The degree of difference between the lightest and darkest parts of a picture.

• The difference or degree of difference between things having similar or comparable natures.

• A comparison of similar objects to set off their dissimilar qualities.

• A person or thing that exhibits differences when compared with another.

Interpreted in a more metaphorical way, our life experiences are enriched, illuminated, edified, and most importantly mirrored by all the other "colors," hues, and differences we encounter.

The front cover imagery of this book is intended to convey these same thoughts. Can you picture yourself if you were one of the little yellow, red, black, or brown dots in a sea of white? The sheer, overpowering nature of the whiteness all around you would probably be overwhelming. Imagine then if the reverse were true and you were white: would you even consider whether there is any significance whatsoever to the colored dots? Would you even be consciously aware of them? I know that, in the first sixty years or so of my life, I never once thought of such questions. Yet, if I were a colored dot, this would be my reality: surrounded and treated as insignificant, or worse.

This is the reality that Black, Indigenous, Latinx/Hispanic, and Asian people have tragically endured for centuries within innumerable deadly circumstances. Just think if the roles were reversed and the cover were multi-colored, with only small white dots instead. And of course, the discussion gets dramatically more complex when you factor in female-male differences, LGBTQIA+ people, the physically challenged, immigrants, refugees, and religion.

There is an unfortunate tendency in today's world to label, if not objectify, people by religion, political affiliation, gender, age, color, etc. So let me begin by identifying myself. In addition to being white, I was born in the United States and am a middle class, tall, seventy-four-year-old Catholic male, cisgender, married to my original spouse, with three children and four grandchildren. I am a registered Independent.

When I first started to write this memoir, it was originally intended to be primarily focused on my own personal journey in the discovery of white privilege. However, as I recollected my youth during the fifties and sixties and began some other research, "white" became much too limiting in my attempt to define "privilege," and things I thought of as specifically white privilege were not. It was not even a concept or a term used at the time — at least not by whites. In fact, white privilege was just one of many other privileges I was born into, which I discovered as I began this writing. For reference, these privileges are listed in the Appendix along with a brief explanation of the important differences between privileges and rights.

I came to discover that my true story was contained within what Merton said above, "that the cancer of injustice and hate which is eating white society and is only partly manifested in racial segregation with all its consequences, is rooted in the heart of the white people themselves." These last few words made me question what those roots were as I was growing up, i.e., what directly or indirectly impacted my heart as a white kid and caused me to shield my eyes from the "cancer of injustice" all around me? Was there anything lacking in my Catholic, pre-Vatican II education that could have better informed me about "racial segregation with all its consequences?

As this memoir will portray, the full awareness of and awakening to the history and impact of racial injustice for me personally was a gradual process and did not begin in earnest until I was sixty-seven years old. This was the true beginning of my late entry into clarity and enlightenment.

It may be hard for many non-whites to understand that unknowingness and obliviousness are pervasive among most whites. A personal illustration of this is when I was involved with a training program on discussing racism. In one exercise, I was paired up with a Black woman a little younger than myself. We were each given three minutes to briefly state how race was discussed when we were growing up. Thankfully, she went first and proceeded to provide a detailed overview of her experience. When it was my turn, I confessed that I literally had nothing to offer. She was surprised, as racial discussions permeated her family life — they were required for survival.

Another revelation occurred as I approached the later decades of writing my life story. I had struggled — consciously or unconsciously, I'm not certain — with using the term white supremacy. It is perhaps the concept which gave birth to and continues to sustain white privilege. Richard Brody, writing in the April 9, 2021, issue of *The New Yorker*, says,

> White supremacy or white supremacism is the belief that white people are superior to those of other races and thus should dominate them. The belief favors the maintenance and defense of white power and privilege. White supremacy has roots in the now-discredited doctrine of scientific racism and was a key justification for colonialism. It also underlies a spectrum of contemporary movements including neo-Confederates and neo-Nazism.

As a sheltered and uninformed white person when it came to matters of race, nothing in my life had prepared me for when I had to confront the concept of white supremacy directly, based on the storyline I was developing of my life's journey. This was further compounded by the continued and seemingly relentless demonstration and displays of white supremacy in our current culture.

Although this memoir is not an extensive autobiography, it follows the course of my life with the intent of identifying some of the many privileges I was born with and subsequently developed and expanded upon in my social and racial awakening. I begin by examining my roots as the product of a white, Catholic, middle-class family and exploring the nature of other personal privileges. Picture the classic Norman Rockwell depiction of the "American Dream" family of six children, with former WWII military parents plus extended family around a holiday table. What might that suggest for the future fulfillment of that overused and, in my opinion, abused term "dream?"

The examination of my life will begin in childhood and then on through the succeeding decades. But first, let me fast forward to the tumultuous year of 2020, since that year provided the catalyst to write about the seeds of my social and racial justice epiphany over the course of my life and my ongoing personal growth.

Based on several e-mail exchanges with some of my relatives in the spring of 2020, during the initial stages of the COVID pandemic and shortly after the police murder of Mr. George Floyd, I thought it would be helpful to provide them some background on my racial and social justice concerns in the form of a self-interview, question-and-answer style. I was hoping that this would be an objective and fair approach to perhaps begin conversations that could lead to a better understanding of each other's beliefs and eventually get into more depth on my own heart's conversion. This personal transformation includes my views on and passion for improving the trajectory of racial and social justice and how our whiteness has impeded this movement towards true equality.

A summary excerpt of one of my e-mails reads as follows: "Bottom line ... the overall journey, similar to my Camino walk, has been remarkable in terms of its interconnectedness, growth, and broadening my view of the world, especially over the past six years. I have moved beyond a lot of my white fragility to better understand how white supremacy and privilege obstructed what I learned in K-16 about truly 'Loving Thy Neighbor' or the 'other.' And I feel blessed to be able to share these thoughts of my journey with you in what, believe it or not, is an abbreviated testimony ... the beauty of which continues to grow including even providing this brief overview. I believe this is what a conversation could look like: i.e., open, honest dialogue where questions can be raised, responses given based on experiences, and with little/no preaching ... at least with words as St. Francis would often say! I hope you each feel the same way."

I concluded with three open-ended questions: "What are your stories and reflections of growing up and continuing to live as a white person in a city, county, state, country, and world with so much and increasing diversity? What do you wish for your children, grandchildren, nieces, nephews, friends in this ever-changing, diverse world? What legacy do you wish to leave that will help them navigate the future perhaps better than we have in our own lives?"

Although I was unsure of the response I would receive, virtual silence was not anticipated. I was struck by the fact that, even though I had shared only a small part of my experience with racial and social justice, there was little reply — and I was left wondering why. Upon deeper reflection, I subsequently reached an awareness that any expectation of responses to the three questions posed to my family members was probably an overreach on my part. Why?

The realization struck me that perhaps I was placing an unsolicited burden on them. Formulating a response could be challenging. Through no fault of their own, based on their upbringing, their experience, and what they were (and were not) taught in our Catholic schools, they and most whites in this country lack what I call a "background of relatedness" to what being white really means. We simply take our whiteness for granted within our embedded notions of white superiority, both consciously and unconsciously.

I took the time to ponder the questions several more times and it dawned on me that there could have been a range of thoughts, from "Huh?" to "I don't want to be bothered." So, instead of possibly opening a dialogue in our overly "siloed" environment due to COVID and other political and social factors, I may have intimidated them by giving the impression that I had predetermined ideas of what the right answers were. It was not my intent to appear "preachy," add stress, or otherwise burden them with things they did not want to discuss or discover about themselves. Based on my personal racial and social justice experience, this is a challenge for most whites, including myself.

A few weeks after that, there were additional responses to two other e-mails I wrote related to my reflections on more police killings of Blacks, related protests, and the rise of the Black Lives Matter (BLM) movement. This time it did generate comments, including "(You are) very offensive;" "How dare you;" "You know very little about America;" "Get off the pulpit;" "You live in a secure neighborhood;" "I'm not falling into your propaganda;" "Your over-the-top bullying is insulting;" "Your followers are lemmings going over the cliff;" "You insist everyone believe what you believe;" "Stop trying to realign my way of thinking to believe in yours;" "I don't get you and this has caused a great divide thanks to you;" "Does your own family know you pass your political views and such crap on us?" "Have not seen you in rallies or protests — what's up with that?"

These comments illustrate the price one may have to pay for simply trying to express one's opinions and represent just a sampling of the divide among some of our beliefs. Given that I pictured the family as rooted within a similar faith system, these responses came as both a surprise and disappointment. However, I knew I was not alone since I occasionally heard some friends' stories of similar encounters within their own families. Other remarks I received included that BLM was a farce, a terrorist group, and Marxist; that I am trying to convert everyone to my supposed socialist/globalization, 'one world order' view (I have to say I don't even know what this means); and several about not being white privileged or privileged in any way. I will attempt to address these comments by simply relating some experiences as to how my perception was transformed over time. This obviously has not been fully revealed to some of my family yet, and perhaps never will be, if their eyes and ears are closed or they are inclined to fabrication.

About the same time as these family exchanges were occurring, I was receiving encouragement from two Black female friends, and a few white friends, to describe my pursuit of social and racial justice by writing a book. Contrary to some of my relatives, these people knew me well and felt that the story of my conversion and change of heart should be told, especially given the increasingly polarized state of our country. They also realized, as did I, that institutions, individuals, and families throughout the country were having similar challenges in discussing different viewpoints. My youngest brother and our youngest son also encouraged me to write.

I want to thank my relatives as well as some other people I care about for the combination of their passive silence and in some cases their words and comments. Either way, they provided inspiration for me to take up the challenge of writing this book so that they and others may get a deeper understanding of my social and racial justice views and how they evolved over the years. My book will further demonstrate that my opinions were not triggered by the tragedies of 2020, but are a product of an inch-by-inch progression over the course of my life, with many sideways and backwards movements, and flaws including sins of commission and omission.

This is a story of my journey from blindness to sight, from deafness to hearing, and from obliviousness to understanding. Hopefully my testimony will be used as a guidepost to help transform other persons irrespective of race, color, or religion as well as provide a positive teaching model to communities of all forms, especially faith communities. Simply writing this memoir has contributed to my own ongoing transformation and I am still on the path of awakening.

Assuming that deeper understanding is not achieved, I would

hope and pray that at minimum there will be a respectful common ground reached where anyone can agree to disagree and have civil conversations. With this as some of the background rationale, the memoir will be focused on the following:

• How my whiteness was the basis for many unearned benefits (privileges) and how I have been blessed with considerable opportunity because of them

• My perspectives on the intersectionality of racism with privilege

• To dig deeper into my personal experience of seeing white privilege as created out of white supremacy, especially white male supremacy

• My developing spirituality and relationship with God through direct connection with "others" despite my slow start in my formative, educational years

• Hopefulness, as derived by my developing a personal conversion of heart through encounter and dialogue

• The convergence of being raised and educated as a Catholic, my gradual awakening to social and racial justice issues, the importance of the Catholic Church's social teaching role, especially regarding racism, and my corollary participation role as a layperson. This gradual awakening is the primary thread, or through line of the book

• That speaking truth to power requires courage and not falling into the trap of being limited by either the complicity of silence or the convenient excuse that social and racial justice issues are political vs. scripturally premised

• That my relatives will begin to understand how the roots of my views, engagement, and advocacy began and evolved to what they are today and that we should be able to "agree to disagree" with love

• My own hopes and personal commitments for the future in the pursuit of the common good

Since I was born in 1947, I start there and then continue with the story of my journey to awareness, participation, and eventual awakening with respect to the discovery of what privilege is and how a correct consciousness about privilege is required for justice and peace.

Finally, I would like to share the following poem:

W.E. WYNNE

Blessed are you
who bear the light
in unbearable times,
who testify
to its endurance
amid the unendurable,
who bear witness
to its persistence
when everything seems
in shadow
and grief.

Blessed are you
in whom
the light lives,
in whom
the brightness blazes —
your heart
a chapel,
an altar where
in the deepest night
can be seen
the fire that
shines forth in you
in unaccountable faith,
in stubborn hope,
in love that illumines
every broken thing
it finds.

(from *Circle of Grace: A Book of Blessings
for the Seasons* by Jan Richardson)

It is my fervent hope that I can continue to fulfill these words in my own life and, via this memoir, describe my attempts to bear witness and illuminate the path for others to follow, no matter whether white; Black, Indigenous, or other People of Color (BIPOC); religious or non-religious — and especially for our youth, the true hope in this world!

Acknowledgments

This book would not have happened without the inspired encouragement of several people.

I dedicated a whole chapter to Fr. Tony Valente, who has continued to be a spirit-filled presence in my life since he passed away in 1995. Tony was there at the beginning of my formal walk on the social and racial justice path, even though I did not realize the true depth of his impact until writing this memoir. Thoughts of him continue to provide encouragement and illumination during my COVID-inspired morning prayer time together with Sandy, where we sit with the print he gave us, "Christ the Liberator," looking over us.

John McDermott, a relatively new friend and a Catholic deacon, was the person who pushed me over the edge by challenging me to utilize and share what he saw were some unique gifts I possessed, based on my social and justice interests and developing activism. What he shared with me in early 2019, shortly after his beloved wife Betsy passed away, was enormous. Within twenty-four hours, a Spirit-induced "call" occurred, which turned out to be the beginning of my activism. Perhaps John was returning the favor of "stepping out" in faith, since I had encouraged him to walk the Camino just the year before. I thank John for his challenge, ongoing support, friendship, and many talks and walks!

There are three Black female friends whom I have previously mentioned in this book, each of whom have provided incredible guidance, insight, support, and friendship. The first is Gaynelle Wethers, whom I have known since 1980, when we were on the CYO Board together. We became fast friends and during the early- to mid-eighties were heavily involved with many agency and diocesan social justice initiatives referenced in Chapter 3. We would see each other occasionally over the ensuing decades but did not talk much until 2012 at a gathering of former Catholic Charities Board members.

This reconnection indirectly helped me attain the CFC development position, which closed out my professional career in 2014.

Then next year, I volunteered to assist in the creation of a new foundation being launched by three large settlement houses in the city. Gaynelle was on the board of one of these (Baden Street) and arranged the introductory meeting with the other two houses to begin making the foundation operational. We stayed in touch and Gaynelle attended the last session of the 2020 SC program at COTA-COR. Then, COVID hit and several circumstances during those early pandemic days led us to have frequent phone conversations regarding a whole host of issues and topics. These included several where Gaynelle provided me encouragement to take on this never-thought-of-before path of being an author. We continue to talk (and conspire!) regularly. I also want to thank her for taking the time to review the second draft of this book and providing helpful comments and suggestions.

Pastor Wanda Wilson was a pastor of a small, Black church in the city whom I met in 2016 while planning and participating in the first Sacred Conversations (SC) program. Pastor Wanda co-facilitated at the downtown church, where she was part of the pastoral staff. Sandy and I stayed in touch, visited her church for Sunday services, went to other events, and then did the same when she became pastor of her own church. She was also a facilitator in both the SC training and MAMA program Sandy and I attended. When Pastor Wanda suggested a second SC program in late 2019, we collaborated and I depended on her experience, wisdom, and call for effective antiracism action. These interactions have led to an enduring friendship, and she continues to inspire me in many ways.

Judy Toyer is the person who virtually insisted that I write this book, and I want to publicly acknowledge and thank her. Her roots are similar to Gaynelle's in that they were both born in Louisiana and raised Catholic, but Judy's roots are more rural and Gaynelle's urban. In Chapter 7 I explained how Judy and I first met at a 2015 Roc/ACTS (R/A) meeting. She had been involved with R/A since its inception a couple of years earlier and was very instrumental in getting the SC program to Rochester. She was also one of the coordinators of the ten-week Black History program so our paths intersected regularly. Judy is a devout Catholic, very spiritually oriented, and our deep conversations usually involved important racial justice topics. We both have learned a lot from and about each other. She provided me edifying wisdom and insight about the overall Black experience, primarily through the sharing of her personal background and trials living in a white supremacist society. Judy was another reviewer of the first two drafts, and I thank her for her critique and suggestions. This memoir would not have happened without her persistent, thoughtful, and Christ-centered encouragement.

Fr. Richard Rohr and his Center for Contemplation and Action are responsible for guiding my spiritual path, which also led to the creation of a small men's group loosely titled the Rohrians. John Notebaert deserves special credit for being the one who introduced me to Rohr. John and I have known each other for over fifty years. He was one of the first two people (the other being Al Wilt) I met upon arriving at St. Bonaventure. Together, with another Bonaventure and McQuaid classmate I want to acknowledge, Ted Naylon, we started our Rohr discussion group in 2015. Ted also provided guidance on the first draft and, since he's an author as well, his assistance on the many aspects of publishing was invaluable.

Rick Micoli, Denis Stemmle, Jim Widboom, Curt Hill, and Claude Adair are also members of our group, with Claude also being a reviewer of the second draft. My deep gratitude to each of these inspiring brothers, with a special shout out to Claude as he was also one of the people who provided initial and ongoing encouragement for me to write this book in the first place.

Denis also warrants acknowledgment for leading me to one of my developmental editors.

Frank Staropoli is another fellow McQuaid alum who warrants a special acknowledgment. Sandy and I have known Frank and his wife Sue for years, including when our kids overlapped in their early school years. In the eighties, Frank asked me to serve on an advisory board of a consulting firm he and another good friend, John Engels, were starting. Our paths continued to intersect, but during the past several years things really got energized.

Frank and I seemingly were on parallel paths in our individual racial justice journeys, with many crossovers — some of which were intentional. A few years ago, he started his "White Guy in Rochester" blog to help educate whites on racism and provide guidance on what becoming an antiracist really means. It has attracted hundreds of local followers and, as described in this memoir, he honored me by asking me to be a contributor for one of his posts.

Frank has toiled unceasingly to increase awareness of racism among whites and readily accepts the critique of Blacks, which I admire since, in our mutual whiteness, we do not have a clue about the Black experience in this country. Therefore, I acknowledge Frank with special appreciation for his inspiring dedication and unfailing commitment in attempting to open the eyes and ears of whites.

There are several other friends who should be recognized who provided direct or indirect support on my journey of social and racial justice over the years. They include Fr. Bob Werth (Bonaventure), Joyce Strazzabosco (CYO), my fellow Camino pilgrims, many Roc/ACTS acquaintances, Steve Jarose (NCBI), Howard Eagle (MAMA and many other initiatives), Shane Wiegand (MAMA and PathStone), the Spiritus Christi community including Fr. Jim Callan and Rev. Myra Brown, and Tiffany Porter (BLM).

I also want to recognize the countless good Sisters of St. Joseph and Sisters of Mercy who have shaped my life since kindergarten. There are way too many to mention, but one deserving of as much recognition as she can get is Sister Grace Miller of the House of Mercy, Rochester's version of Mother Theresa, together with Sister Rita.

I am not going to mention any individual names, but there are several Fairport/Perinton government and school leaders with whom I have interacted over the past couple of years. I am very grateful for their responsiveness and guidance in helping me express my social and racial justice voice on important local matters.

In both the Preface and Afterword, I acknowledged the importance of my relatives in moving me to write this memoir. I am very grateful for them being such a large part of my life. And I would be remiss if I did not give a special acknowledgment and heartfelt appreciation to my youngest brother, Tim. This is not only for his encouragement, but primarily for his willingness and openness to discuss hard topics and have meaningful conversations. I am forever grateful.

A special thanks to our children, Allyson, Sean, and Andrew, who each provided moral support whether they knew it or not. Without any overt direction or prodding on my part, they are living their lives and providing the modeling for their children, nieces, and nephews that is greatly influencing their social and racial justice development in thoughts, words, and actions. Our youngest son, Andrew, was especially present and supportive at my deliberative stage when I was questioning whether I should take on the task of writing a book or not. They are each an inspiration for me, as well our grandchildren Jack, Ava, Hudson, and Harper, who are the future, hopeful pilgrims on their own paths in fostering justice in the world.

None of this would have been possible, however, without my life partner, Sandy, my wife, mother of our children, "Nana" to her grandchildren, aunt, sister, niece, cousin, caregiver, and close friend and confidant to countless others. The courage Sandy demonstrated in our early years has carried forward through the decades. We have walked many challenging paths together, including the Camino, but none so transformative as our racial justice journey of the past several years. I can honestly say I do not think I could have accomplished what I have without Sandy by my side.

To be able to share our experiences, perspectives, and individual stories has been a blessing. She was also the first to review the initial draft of this memoir and her comments and critiques were invaluable. I know many of her close friends would consider her a unique person. When we first got married, I used to call her "Nique" for being just that, and I am privileged that she has allowed me to be a part of that specialness which resonates in everything she does!

I was blessed to have both Krista Hill of L Talbot Editorial Services and Paul J. Hoffman and his entire team at PathBinder Publishing as my editor and publisher, respectively. Their guidance, support, and professional expertise were tremendously important as was their unwavering faith in the importance of this book. They both have become friends for life.

Three other people who should be recognized are George McGuire of Bond, Schoeneck & King, PLLC who provided legal advice; Devin Mack, owner of DFUNLIFE Photography, for my photo; and Wil Johnson, of TsTi Cyber Solutions, for his work on my website.

I could go on mentioning many other friends and colleagues who have been an important part of my life's journey. You know who you are, and if you choose to read this memoir, I trust it is somewhat consistent with what you know about me, even though it probably contains a few surprises as well. Some of you should be glad it wasn't a more in-depth autobiography, otherwise there could have been a few more interesting revelations!

I am extremely grateful for your friendship! Love and peace to you all!

Contents

Part I
Chapter 1
1940s and 1950s: Whiteness

PEXELS

A depiction of whiteness.

"Whiteness is not only false and oppressive; it is nothing but false and oppressive." (David R. Roediger, Towards the Abolition of Whiteness: Essays on Race, Politics, and Working Class History)

"No label, no slogan, no party, no skin color, and no religion is more important than the human being." (James Baldwin)

"'So the real question would be,' he said finally, 'if people were given the choice between democracy and whiteness, how many would choose whiteness?'" (Taylor Branch, as quoted by Isabel Wilkerson in Caste -The Origins of Our Discontents)

PEOPLE AND EVENTS IN THE NEWS, 1947-1959: Gandhi, Chung Kai-shek, Truman, Marshall Plan, Pakistan & India, CIA, Jackie Robinson, WHO, Israel, South Africa/Apartheid, NATO, Eisenhower, Interstate Highways, Redlining, Korea, Atomic Bomb drills, Cold War, McCarthy, Civil Rights, Rosa Parks, MLK, Emmett Till, Vietnam, Polio, Salk vaccine, Native American Right to Vote

I was born in Rochester, New York, on January 19, 1947, which is also Confederate General Robert E. Lee's birthday. Lee is a somewhat paradoxical historical figure to be personally connected with, given his role in trying to preserve white supremacy contrasted with my eventual awakening decades later regarding how this dangerous ideology has continued to endure. In contrast, sometimes Martin Luther King Jr. Day falls on January 19: that is a more ideal or "dream" connection, so to speak.

My parents had moved from New York City to Rochester, where my mother was born and raised, several months prior in 1946, shortly after my father's brother Bill died. I was named after him in his memory and was probably conceived shortly after his death. My father and uncle were extremely close and, with his brother's passing, my father was the sole remaining member of his immediate family.

They grew up in Stamford, Connecticut, outside New York City, and both my uncle and my father became undertakers. My parents met while serving in the Navy during World War II, were married in 1945, then lived in New York City after their military discharges.

After moving to Rochester, my father bought a funeral home on Park Avenue in the city with a $10,000 mortgage (more on this later). I am the eldest of six children and we all lived upstairs over the funeral home until 1969. My father passed away in 1966, when I was a junior in college, causing my stay-at-home mom to return to nursing. Mom was descended from second-generation German immigrants and Dad from first-generation Irish immigrants.

I was baptized in Blessed Sacrament Church, which was close by in the city and thus began a conventional Roman Catholic upbringing and education. My parents were very well known and involved in the life of the parish. All the priests and nuns knew us, but as a family of six children we were left in the dust compared to several other families of eight to ten children or more. It was a period of wonderful simplicity in an almost (probably 100 percent) all-white neighborhood, although I never thought about it that way growing up, since everyone I knew was white.

"Whiteness" was implicit, embedded, and not even a concept. Perfect obliviousness! Black and white TV was also effectively all-white in content, context, and performers. The pope was white; politicians and baseball players were virtually all white; all our teachers were white. John Wayne and even Tarzan were white! I loved to watch their movies on TV and was enthralled when the Indian "savages" were killed by the soldiers, and when the Black brutes were outsmarted by the white Tarzan. Everything around me at an early age conspired to inform me that people of color (with whom I never had an interaction) were mysterious individuals to be avoided.

Another example of whiteness ubiquity at the time can be seen in a video depicting Life magazine photos from the 1950s and 1960s showing us "what summer in America used to look like." You can see the video at https://biggeekdad.com/2020/03/1950s-and-1960s-summer-photos. Note that every single one of the people in the photos is white and the irony that the song being played is sung by Nat King Cole, a Black man.

The Park Avenue area where I was born and raised was vastly different from the trendy, diverse, youthful neighborhood it is today. In the forties and fifties, neighborhoods were heavily concentrated with white ethnicities, including those of German and Irish descent like my parents. The atmosphere was vibrant but in a colorless, post-WWII sort of way, where the suburban growth (and white flight) of the sixties had not yet taken over.

I do not even recollect a Black person simply walking in our neighborhood, other than perhaps city or service workers. If that had happened, my reaction would probably have been one of surprise but not much more than that since we were only a couple of miles from downtown, where I would see Black people out and about. There would never be any direct engagement with Blacks other than perhaps in stores where they may have worked.

Essentially, the implicit messaging I grew up with was that

Blacks were different, that silence was observed if anything like race entered a conversation, and that being white was something we absolutely did not even have to think about. Therefore, a concept such as "white privilege" would not even have been thought of. But there were other class distinctions prevalent at the time, taught even by my teachers at Blessed Sacrament.

A memory that I have of my K-8 parochial education, besides being in a school with all white students and taught by white nuns and lay teachers, is the after-school religious education classes that were held in our classrooms for Catholic kids who attended nearby city public schools. They came once a week for religion classes after the regular school day. Our teachers would usually advise us on those days before we left the classroom to hide or take home anything of value from our desks. An attitude was burnt into our young, developing, Catholic-educated minds about being cautious of the 'other,' including those kids who were probably neighborhood friends in many cases and went to the same church on Sundays. Perhaps this was just a minor matter of class differentiation, i.e., parochial versus public students, but nonetheless it provided an instance of privilege and bias for me at an early age, though not recognized until much later in life.

Catholic grade school religious curriculum at the time relied heavily on studying and memorization of what was known as the "Baltimore Catechism." This was the official, national school text for Catholic children in the country from 1885 to the late 1960s. Its focus as I recall was more on the Ten Commandments and avoidance of sin as contrasted with the Eight Beatitudes' emphasis on love of neighbor (or the 'other').

Teaching was premised more on what I would suggest was an 'observer' basis of Christ's life versus developing a better understanding as to who Jesus really was and how to experience His humanity in our own lives. His divinity was more emphasized than His mortal life. He suffered, died on the cross, and ascended into heaven, never to be seen again but with promises of a future "coming." Therefore, it seemed as if mankind was left on its own, with whispers from the Spirit, revelations in the form of apparitions and miracles, and access to the sacraments while being led by priests, prophets, mystics, and saints. All showed us the way to fulfill Jesus' challenge to "build my Church."

What was lacking in this passive approach to understanding who Jesus really was and what His life really meant? What teaching opportunity was missed when it came to comprehending the full wisdom contained in the parables versus literal interpretations? For an answer to these questions, I draw upon the parable of the Good Samaritan, which Pope Francis beautifully describes in chapter two of his recent encyclical letter, "*Fratelli Tutti.*"[1]

Pope Francis included the words "other(s)" and "another" twenty-four times in this chapter, as well as many "Samaritan-like" euphemisms and terms including stranger, needy, sojourner, foolish, scapegoats, foreigners, lepers, orphan, widow, marginalized, weak, illiterate, frail, vulnerable, suffering, fallen, outcast, wounded, poor, injured, stranded, impure, detestable, dangerous and, lastly, neighbor. In general, all these terms describe or represent our "neighbors." Pope Francis also states later in the chapter that "... the words of Jesus ... compel us to recognize Christ himself in each of our abandoned or excluded brothers and sisters." *(cf. Mt25:40,45)*

The full import of this perception of Christ as a "Stranger on the Road" was not effectively brought home to me in my formative schooling. I was taught to be a listener, an observer, and a bystander of a story about kindness and charity, and not to look at it as a way to know Jesus through "others" and their cries for justice. We were merely expected to emulate Jesus' good works and not necessarily to dig deeper as to why acts of charity were necessary in the first place.

Even though this was a good place to start, I eventually understood that the *only* way to know and have a relationship with Jesus in this life is through authentic, caring, and empathetic relationships

---

1 Translation: "Brothers All." The chapter is aptly titled "A Stranger on the Road" and I strongly encourage Catholics and non-Catholics alike to read its short fourteen pages if not the entire letter. My rationale in referencing Pope Francis' reflections on this famous parable is that it contains the answers to the two questions at the beginning of this paragraph.

with "others" and not to be a bystander or, even worse, the "robber," as portrayed in the parable of the Good Samaritan.

With that thought in mind, take a moment and ask yourself the question as to which character you relate to most in this story. What are your own recollections of this parable when you were growing up or, more importantly, how does this story make you feel today? This is a question that should be discussed in today's classrooms, from the pulpit, and among followers of other faiths and humanists who value the democratic principles of liberty, justice, and equality. Simply stated, this is not a question limited to Christian teaching and can be used to engage in reflection on racial justice for people of all faiths.

My personal feeling, as Pope Francis suggested in his letter, is that we have likely related to each of the characters at one time or another in our lives. Therefore, I realized that I have a lot to learn and "miles to go before I sleep." The through line of this narrative as it progresses will focus on my transition from the baseline of attempting to do good works for the "Samaritans" in my life to the evolution of building relationships with my neighbors to fully understand the injustices they routinely face. As the parable concludes, "Go and do likewise!"

This is how a social and racial justice advocacy journey begins, but it is a hard road even for the Catholic Church, our country, and the world, as the pope describes in Paragraph 86 of *Fratelli Tutti:*

> I sometimes wonder why, in light of this (the plea of the "stranger") it took so long for the Church unequivocally to condemn slavery and various forms of violence. Today, with our developed spirituality and theology, we have no excuses. Still, there are those who appear to feel encouraged or at least permitted by their faith to support varieties of narrow and violent nationalism, xenophobia and contempt, and even the mistreatment of those who are different. For this reason, it is important that catechesis and preaching speak more directly and clearly about the social meaning of existence, the fraternal dimension of spirituality, our conviction of the inalienable dignity of each person, and our reasons for loving and accepting *all our brothers and sisters.*

To dig a little deeper into the more religious aspects of my upbringing, most Catholics — and perhaps non-Catholics — would start with describing the Mass, since it is the central liturgical rite in the Catholic Church. It encompasses the Liturgy of the Word and the Liturgy of the Eucharist, where the bread and wine are consecrated and become the Body and Blood of Christ. The Latin Mass and all other liturgical ceremonies were in the pre-Vatican II traditional, centuries-old style and thus had many long-established "pomp and circumstance" components that typified Catholic liturgies.

A little more history: this form of liturgical experience was the norm until the Second Vatican Council i.e. "Vatican II" of 1962-65, called by Pope John XXIII and eventually concluded by Pope Paul VI after Pope John's death. This convening of key, world-wide Catholic leadership (the majority of whom were white male prelates) brought about needed change to better position the Church within the modern world and strongly promoted more laity involvement.

But these fruits and others brought about by Vatican II were realized well after the roots of my Catholic foundation had been firmly established. Unfortunately, what I was taught in my grade school days prior to Vatican II included hardly anything connected to social justice topics. Therefore, I was limited in my understanding of the importance of the Church's role in these matters and did not grasp the full significance of concepts like "justice for all" for many years. This gap in social justice education was identified as a deficiency by Church leaders at the time, and Pope John and the Council subsequently addressed it by placing more emphasis on issues such as basic human rights for all in its final documents.

I will have more to say about my view of the Catholic Church's social and racial justice teachings in this country as this narrative continues. An interesting footnote is that, for a year or two after I graduated from college, I taught an elementary grade level of religious education on Sundays at the school my younger brothers attended, so for a brief period I was part of the system.

Besides being baptized at Blessed Sacrament, through the course of my grade school days I also had the sacraments of Penance (confession of sins), First Communion, and Confirmation. Years later,

I was married there. In eighth grade I was also encouraged by my teacher to consider entering the seminary to become a priest. After some personal reflection and discussion with my parents, I decided not to go that route. I also pondered becoming a deacon in the early eighties. Though I had several close friends who were deacons, I did not pursue the deaconate and I have no regrets. If I had, my life would have been profoundly different, and I probably would not be writing this memoir.

My parents were both raised Roman Catholic and, as mentioned, their ancestral roots were German (my mother) and Irish (my father). Even though we were raised Catholic, if it had not been for both of my grandmothers, we could have easily been raised Lutheran or perhaps Episcopalian. Although I am not clear on the circumstances, my maternal grandmother, who came from a devout Lutheran family, converted to Catholicism prior to marrying my grandfather. My father's mother was Irish Catholic and left Ireland to marry my grandfather, who was Protestant and living in the US. My father and his two siblings were raised as Catholics. Due to these circumstances, both my parents were Catholic and so were their children. Additionally, as first- and second-generation immigrants, it is likely that their parents suffered some forms of discrimination, but since the "melting pot" at the time worked reasonably well if one was of a white ethnicity, any overt prejudice probably dissipated over time.

My siblings' and my educations were very important to our parents, and we were all encouraged to excel academically and participate in school activities. During my later elementary years, I was an altar server, choir boy, member of the safety patrol, and I participated in many school musicals, plays, and other activities. Our neighborhood was also high energy: there were many children of the Baby Boomer generation living on adjoining streets. Summers were jam-packed with all sorts of street or sandlot ballgames (sometimes on the gravel in our rear parking area) and other activities morning, noon, and night. We had a large backyard, so our house was a big draw for our friends.

But again, there were some exclusionary elements as well to our neighborhood life. For example, there was a large apartment building adjacent to us, but we were encouraged by our parents not to mingle with the kids who lived there. Whether we abided by that is another matter, as I recall bypassing the house rules myself.

My involvement with school and church life on the Blessed Sacrament campus eventually provided me access to various student leadership roles, such as president of the boys choir for two years (contrary to the traditional one year), being chosen for several choral solos, and being selected to head up the school safety patrol. I reference these roles not to flaunt any special talent or merit on my part but to perhaps suggest that my parents' overall presence and involvement, along with their owning a business, might have provided me a "leg up" (privilege?) vis-à-vis others who might have been even more qualified.

Perhaps these opportunities were not byproducts of privilege and to state this as such is an overreach; nonetheless, these roles provided me access to those in charge of the school, were foundational building blocks, and the experience as well as the resulting leadership responsibilities were formative to my development.

As mentioned, my father strongly advocated for me to excel academically and sometimes referred to me as "Doctor," to my chagrin. He would go so far as to state his thoughts on my potential, future career as a doctor or lawyer. Although not a natural student or athlete, I studied hard, played sports, and was usually at the top of my class — but there were several girls way ahead of most of us guys!

One memory I have was winning the right to represent Blessed Sacrament in the annual McQuaid Jesuit High School spelling bee. The top prize was a full, four-year scholarship to this all-boys school (otherwise it probably would have been a girl who won the opportunity). I think I really disappointed my father by getting knocked out in the second round, ironically (in hindsight years later) by the word "foreigner." He was adamant that both my brother and I attend this relatively new Jesuit school that was not too far away from where we lived, so "losing" that scholarship did not really matter.

Since I was the oldest of six siblings, my father would at times position me as the surrogate "authority" as I got older. I did not ask for this honor and, as a young person myself, it was easy to take advantage — but I do not think I abused it. If I had, I do recall something about a wooden spoon. Thankfully my mother tempered these situations.

People are often interested in my life living above a funeral home. My mother and we four older siblings helped my father in different ways (e.g., setting up for calling hours, bringing in flowers, playing the "Rock of Ages" record during funerals, and more. It was definitely a family business. I carry memories of my father's authentic demonstration of empathy in his ministry of service to bereaved families. Given my father's New York mortician experience, he had many skills and abilities that other local undertakers did not have, and he would often be called upon for assistance.

The embalming room was right off a large, two-car garage and the funeral home itself, including my father's office, took up the whole first floor. Our friends were typically wary of coming into the house, especially since the most direct way was through the embalming room! But there were two other access points to our living quarters. Having lived in the house since birth, I gave little thought to the uniqueness of my living situation, nor did I have any qualms. That said, I was not inspired to become an undertaker.

Although it is hard for me to recall my parents' exact political leanings, I am fairly certain they favored the Republican Party, given that they both served in the US Navy in WWII and the fifties were the Eisenhower years. They were both active in the American Legion. The 1960 election changed the political dynamic with Catholics across the country, especially for my father, given that an Irish Catholic Democrat was running for President. My mother always worked in the neighborhood voting site on primary and election days, and we would occasionally visit her there. With her experience and her patriotic spirit, it would be interesting to get her perspective on the voter suppression movements going on throughout the country today.

As I mentioned previously, my neighborhood was a virtually all white section of the city. This was due to a couple of important historical facts. First, the Great Migration of southern Blacks was just beginning to impact Rochester, so there were not that many Blacks living in

Rochester in the late forties. Eventually, they would come by the thousands — after WWII, in the fifties — in search of jobs and to escape the terrors of "Jim Crow." Rochester hit its historical peak population in 1950 at ~332,000, but its Black population was only around 8,000 (2 percent). It should be noted that, in 2020, the Black population in the city was ~ 88,000 versus a greatly reduced overall population of ~ 210,000, or 41 percent, representing a 20x Black population percentage increase and a large Latinx/Hispanic presence as well.

Secondly, the systemic racist practice of redlining flourished in Rochester, as it did in virtually every community in the country, thereby limiting housing access to just a few city wards for people of color (POC). Redlining is the discriminatory practice of denying services (typically financial) to residents of certain areas based on their race or ethnicity. Park Avenue, where I lived, and the streets parallel to it were a virtual "gated community," including thousands of houses and apartments. Various insidious housing access practices continued to endure due to redlining.

Three important terms (de jure segregation, de facto discrimination, redlining) will help illuminate what happened to cause the Great Migration in the first place and the resulting responses in northern and western cities across the nation, including Rochester.

De jure segregation refers specifically to discriminatory segregation imposed or allowed by government-enacted laws, regulations, or accepted public policy such as Jim Crow laws in the South and the apartheid system in South Africa.

Jim Crow laws were state and local laws that enforced racial segregation in the southern United States. They were enacted in the late 19th and early 20th centuries by white-dominated southern state legislatures to disenfranchise Blacks by removing any political or economic gains made during the Reconstruction period after the Civil War. Such laws were enforced until 1965.

When Blacks migrated out of the South by the thousands in the early to mid-1900s to escape the routine horror and trauma of Jim Crow, they were then faced with its Northern cousin, de facto discrimination, meaning discrimination in practice but not necessarily ordained by law. This brought about the Northern version of segregation and was based on supposed societal differences between groups, without much if any institutionalized legislation intended to segregate. Redlining is one of the sinister results of de facto discrimination. For more information on redlining, go to: https://www.redfin.com/blog/redlining-real-estate-racial-wealth-gap. The next two paragraphs are excerpts from a presentation by a local public-school teacher, Shane Wiegand, and will shed light on how de facto discrimination worked in Rochester and still does to this day.

From the 1920s until 1956, the Code of Ethics set by the National Association of Real Estate Boards stated: "A realtor should never be instrumental in introducing into a neighborhood a character of property or occupancy, members of any race or nationality, or any individuals whose presence will clearly be detrimental to property values in that neighborhood."

In 1954, teacher Dr. Walter Cooper describes what this looked like in practice: "I then confronted the housing segregation in Rochester when my wife and I answered ads for sixty-nine apartments and were refused at all of them."

Another teacher, Alice Young, and her husband attempted to buy a house on Millbank Street in the 19th ward. After a real estate agent would not arrange the sale, they had a white person buy it and transfer them the deed. Shortly thereafter they received a letter threatening to burn the house down. It was signed, "KKK of Millbank Street." Mrs. Georgianna Sibley, the last Sibley family member to live in the Sibley Mansion at 400 East Avenue, took this young promising teacher under her wing and helped guide her career as she blossomed into a community leader.

Dr. Young has shared that it was Mrs. Sibley who served as a surrogate homebuyer for the Young family. She bought the house the Youngs wanted and then sold it to them. All across Rochester and suburbs like Brighton, Pittsford, Penfield, and Irondequoit there were special rules written into the legal document that proved a person owned their land. One of these rules was called a 'restrictive covenant.' A restrictive covenant was a rule that said no people of color were legally allowed to buy or live in the house above the land."As we grew up during this period, my siblings and I were completely oblivious to these exclusionary systems. They were hidden in practice and never discussed. Similarly, there were never conversations about race in our family that I can recall, basically because every institution in our lives was white. At Blessed Sacrament, we were also educated completely in white-oriented history and themes, as were all students at the time, whether public or private.

When I reflect on why there was no response from most of my relatives to the three questions mentioned previously in the Preface, I begin to realize that I am perhaps placing an unfair burden on them due to the totality of our white upbringing during those formative years. Our family, friends, neighborhood, classmates, schooling, and early growing-up experiences included no one of color that I recall. That does not necessarily preclude the impact of other later life experiences with people of color, but during our formative years we were completely uninformed and segregated. Society not only condoned this but regulated it systemically, as described above in the discussion on de facto segregation.

Essentially, we (at least the four oldest) were denied the opportunities of diversity experiences during the fifties and were otherwise ignorant. Did that make our parents, other adult relatives and friends, priests, teachers, etc., bad people for not informing us or broadening the dialogue? Obviously not, since they were all participating in the same system that they had grown up with. It was not until the sixties that things began to change dramatically, and then, unfortunately, misunderstandings and tensions began to arise.

I conclude with a reflection formed from a question I pose similarly at the end of each chapter: Using the lens of my life experience, what words of advice would I give today to my almost thirteen-year-old self at the conclusion of this decade?

As it turns out, that's close to the same age of our oldest grandchild, so I will answer this as if I were speaking to him as well as our other grandchildren. The ability to get information on important topics such as racism is completely different today due to the many diverse forms of media and communication available. Therefore, I would strongly encourage my younger self as well as my grandson to seek out two or three adult "filters" in the form of parents, other elder relatives, or a favorite teacher and have conversations about subjects of interest where I might have questions.

It would have been interesting given the societal norms of the time predicated on whiteness to see how a racism-oriented question might have been perceived. At least pursuing it as an intellectual curiosity beyond the classroom would have provided some guidance for similar questions and discussions at a later age.

Later in this book I will tell a brief story about my eleven-year-old grandson, who did raise a question to his mother about racism last year during the pandemic. There is hope for the future!

Lastly, please take a moment to refer to the last quote at the beginning of this chapter and reflect on what your response might be. It is a very provocative question, so be mindful of your answer as you continue reading.

Chapter 2
1960s: A Cacophony of Change

AUTHOR SUBMISSION
The author, on his college graduation day in 1968 with his aunt.

"One cannot deny the humanity of another without diminishing one's own." (James Baldwin)

"Freedom is never voluntarily given by the oppressor; it must be demanded by the oppressed." (Rev. Martin Luther King Jr.)

"It is a truth of the world's major religions that the goal of God's work — God by any name, I might add — is always healing reconciliation and not retributive justice, resurrection and not death." (Fr. Richard Rohr, March 30, 2021)

PEOPLE AND EVENTS IN THE NEWS, 1960-1969: The Great Society, Vietnam, Vatican II, civil rights, JFK, MLK, RFK, Malcolm X, protests, Watts, Rochester, and Detroit, Algiers Motel, Black Power, Woodstock, Chicago Convention, Stonewall, Tet, Neil Armstrong, equal pay, voting rights, housing rights, Birmingham, Montgomery, draft, LBJ, Nixon, Missile Crisis, Bay of Pigs, Goldwater, Che Guevara, Betty Friedan, Super Bowl, Baldwin, "Bridge Over Troubled Water," urban renewal, American Indian Movement (AIM), Cassius Clay/Muhammad Ali

I am going to begin this chapter with an experience that occurred the summer between my junior and senior years at McQuaid, when I was selected as a delegate to Boys State by my parents' American Legion post. Founded in 1935 by the Legion, Boys State is a week-long educational program of government instruction in which male high school students throughout the country learn the rights, privileges, and responsibilities of citizens. Each state has its own program and the training centers on the structure of city, county, and state governments. It is student-operated and includes elections to various offices. I recall being appointed an assistant district attorney — that probably pleased my father. Program activities included legislative sessions, court proceedings, law-enforcement presentations, assemblies, bands, choruses, and recreational programs. Several observations stand out as I recollect this experience:

• First, the all-male nature of the program. Despite the American Legion Auxiliary sponsoring a similar program for high school girls, called Girls State, it was separate. Boys State remains operational today, as well as Boys Nation, where two delegates from each State conference are chosen to attend

• I question why this gender separation continues in the 21st century; more diversity of thought and political understanding among genders could be achieved by integrating these programs

• In looking at the photos now on their respective websites, both programs continue to be overwhelmingly white in terms of both its adult leadership and student participants

• One of my earliest contacts with a person of color was a Black delegate from another local Legion post, whom I met on the bus transporting us to Colgate University. He was the son of a prominent local family, tall, outgoing, and self-assured. There were hundreds of boys from across the state who attended, and I cannot recall any other contact we may have had that week. This was not due to any consciously intended avoidance of him or other Blacks who may have been there, but strictly due to the logistical circumstances. Not

46

until I went to college was I to have more personal connections with Blacks, but even those were limited.

• As I reflect on discussions with some of my high school and college classmates over the years, unsurprisingly their experiences were virtually identical to mine. Is it any wonder that we were oblivious to the Black experience or, more importantly, that we question whether any avoidance was intentional or caused by unconscious bias? A tough question for whites today is whether we make a conscious decision to perpetuate avoidance and bias, as today it is a real choice with the innumerable examples of racism in our midst. What I now have come to realize and appreciate is how my life would have been enriched had I, with intentionality, reached out more to the "other."

Since the complex dynamics of the sixties represent several fundamental aspects of my grounding as well as my failure to acknowledge the diverse, changing social environment, I want to introduce Fr. Richard Rohr for those who may not be aware of him. He has had a tremendous influence on my spiritual life since 2013, and though this chapter is about the sixties, I thought I would share some of his life and journey, which somewhat parallels mine.

Very briefly, Richard Rohr, Order of Friars Minor (OFM), is an American author, spiritual writer, and Franciscan friar based in Albuquerque, New Mexico, and founder of the Center for Action and Contemplation (CAC). He was ordained to the priesthood in the Roman Catholic Church in 1970. PBS has called him "one of the most popular spirituality authors and speakers in the world." One note: although his popularity, even among non-Catholics, is rapidly increasing, he's hardly your everyday priest!

To quote directly from his Aug. 24, 2020, daily reflection titled *"Order, Disorder, Reorder: The Ability to Hold Paradox"* (see appendix for definitions):

> I began as a very conservative pre-Vatican II Roman Catholic, living in 1940s and 1950s Kansas, pious and law abiding, buffered and bounded by my parents' stable marriage and many lovely liturgical traditions that sanctified my time and space. This was my first wonderful simplicity or period of Order. I was a very happy child and young man, and all who knew me then would agree. Yet, I grew in my experience and

was gradually educated in the much larger world of the 1960s and 1970s, with degrees in philosophy and theology, and a broad liberal arts education given me by the Franciscans. That education was the second journey into rational complexity and critical thinking. I had to leave the garden, just as Adam and Eve had to do (Genesis 3:23–24), even though my new Scripture awareness made it obvious that Adam and Eve were probably not historical figures, but important archetypal symbols. Darn it! I was heady with knowledge and enlightenment and was surely not in Kansas anymore. I had passed, like Dorothy, "over the rainbow." It is sad and disconcerting for a while outside the garden, and some lovely innocence dies in this time of Disorder. Many will not go there, precisely because it is a loss of seeming "innocence" — things learned at our "Mother's knee," as it were.

As time passed, I became simultaneously very traditional and very progressive, and I have probably continued to be so to this day. I found a larger and even happier garden (note the new garden described at the end of the Bible in Revelation 21!). I fully believe in Adam and Eve now, but on about ten more levels. (Literalism is usually the lowest and least level of meaning.) I no longer fit in with either staunch liberals or strict conservatives. This was my first strong introduction to paradox, and it honed my ability to hold two seemingly opposite positions at the same time. It took most of midlife to figure out what had happened — and how and why it had to happen.

This "pilgrim's progress" was, for me, sequential, natural, and organic as the circles widened, and as I taught in more and more countries. While the solid ground of the perennial tradition never really shifted, I found that the lens, the criteria, the inner space, and the scope continued to expand. I was always being moved toward greater differentiation and larger viewpoints, and simultaneously toward a greater inclusivity in my ideas, a deeper understanding of people, and a more honest sense of justice. God always became bigger and led me to bigger places.

This reflection is distinctly personal, meaningful, and somewhat similar in my own life, which will be further demonstrated as this story moves into later decades. Fr. Richard's *Order, Disorder, Reorder* (ODR) sequences and patterns occur to us throughout our lifetimes, and most of us, including myself, usually fail to realize not only the ebbs and flows of these patterns but also the significance of this natural and recurring phenomena.

I was cautioned, however, by a reviewer of this book early on that the majority of BIPOC might see this ODR cycle quite differently in that "disorder" typically and overwhelmingly prevails in their lives. Perhaps it's another matter of privilege to be able to even consider that there is this form of harmony in the universe.

To continue, Rohr's first paragraph in the reflection above that he "grew in my experience and was gradually educated in a much larger world of the 1960s" presents an interesting juxtaposition for how I was educated in the Catholic tradition. My personal recollection of elementary, secondary, and undergraduate schools is that their curricula did not include the full and accurate accounts of Black and Native American histories in this country and were taught solely from a white perspective. This remains true today, according to my children.

Furthermore, there was very little teaching about Catholic social and racial justice (versus being engaged in acts of charity), beginning with the good Sisters of St. Joseph at Blessed Sacrament at the elementary level, followed by the Jesuits at McQuaid in high school, and then the Franciscans at St. Bonaventure University. It is no wonder, therefore, that I and most young Catholics at the time were ill-prepared for understanding society's clamoring call for justice, freedom, and equality, beginning in the sixties. This lack of knowledge and insight bound me to rely primarily on my very inadequate white perspective for many decades to follow. My fear is that similar educational and experiential gaps in connection with the true history and prevailing injustices of this country continue to influence the youth of today.

St. Bonaventure provided some academic and experiential breakthroughs, since its Franciscan philosophy and theology are premised on that of its founder, Saint Francis of Assisi, one of the most venerated figures in Christianity. I then was introduced to another Franciscan, the aforementioned Fr. Rohr, years later through the advice of one of my first classmates I met when I started at St. Bonaventure. A convergence of my educational past with the Jesuits and Franciscans came about on a world-wide scale with the first Jesuit becoming pope in 2013. He is the first pope to take the Saint Francis name.

The Franciscans and Jesuits are religious orders that serve the Catholic Church in similar yet different ways from other Catholic priests and religious orders. A religious order is comprised of communities of people who live apart from society in accordance with their specific religious devotion, usually characterized by the principles of its founder's religious practice.

For example, the Franciscan tradition believes that lifestyle and practice (orthopraxy) are considerably more important than doctrines or theory (orthodoxy); i.e., that life is more important than doctrine. The Jesuits were founded by St. Ignatius of Loyola in 1540 and have been esteemed educators for centuries. They believe that their prime educational objective must be to form men and women "for others," i.e., men and women who will live not for themselves but for God and his Christ. McQuaid's mantra for many years was, "Men for Others." In many ways, I was blessed to be a product of both educational traditions.

Consistent with my elementary education (but perhaps I was not paying attention), both McQuaid and Bonaventure provided little depth regarding the Catholic Church's social and racial justice teaching — but they were hardly alone. In fact, it was not until 1973 that Fr. Pedro Arrupe, the well-known Jesuit and former superior general of the Jesuits, said in an address entitled *Men and Women for Others*:

> Education for justice has become in recent years one of the chief concerns of the Church. Why? Because there is a new awareness in the Church that participation in the promotion of justice and the liberation of the oppressed is a constitutive element of the mission which Our Lord has entrusted to her. Impelled by this awareness, the Church is now engaged in a massive effort to education — or rather to re-educate — herself, her children, and all men and women so that we may all lead our life in its entirety in accord with the evangelical principles of personal and social morality to be expressed in a living Christian witness.

I would go as far as to say that, in my view, Fr. Arrupe's vision expressed almost fifty years ago remains largely unfulfilled in the Catholic Church today. It simply has not been taught and preached as it should have been, notwithstanding the United States Catholic Conference of Bishops' (USCCB) attempts over the years to raise consciousness among Catholics concerning the importance of social and racial justice teaching. The USCCB has said this continues to be a big challenge in the Church, and it is worthy of note since we are well into the post-Vatican II era of supposed great change.

Religious education at Bonaventure was an academic requirement every semester. I cannot recall too many details on the content, but two experiences come to mind. There must have been a course on biblical interpretation, and I remember telling my mother when I was home for break that the story of Noah's Ark was probably a metaphorical account and never really happened. I don't think she was very happy to hear that and no doubt wondered what else I was learning at the school her Franciscan cousin had recommended.

The second incident was in the second semester of my senior year in 1968. The Franciscan teacher, Fr. Francis Xavier (otherwise known as Frannie X) was one who had taught me several times before. He was also our class moderator/chaplain and I always thought it interesting that, as a Franciscan, he took the name of a famous Jesuit saint, Francis Xavier. This parallels our current Jesuit pope, who took the name of the famous Franciscan saint and founder of the Franciscans — another model of Jesuit and Franciscan integration!

In any event, the pope at the time was rumored to be writing an encyclical opposing birth control, and Fr. Francis predicted vigorously that the pope would not do that. Well, he did, and I knew based on how principled Fr. Francis was that his life as a Franciscan was probably over. I was right: he left the Franciscan order and got married. Such were the times in the raucous sixties!

A recollection I have about my spiritual development at Bonaventure relates to several philosophy courses I took exposing me to new ways of seeing the world, especially through the words of authors such as Herman Hesse. His famous novel, *Siddhartha,* tells the story of a young man who leaves his family for a contemplative life. Becoming restless, he discards it for one of the flesh. He has a son, but bored and sickened by lust and greed he moves on again. Near despair, Siddhartha comes to a river, where he hears a unique sound.

51

This sound signals the true beginning of his life and the beginning of suffering, rejection, peace, and finally, wisdom.

The river is one of the most potent symbols in the entire book and one I occasionally reflect upon. It symbolizes not only the journey towards enlightenment, which is the goal of Siddhartha throughout his life, but also the realization of enlightenment itself. I have read this short book many times over the years and its varied messages always speak to me in new ways. If you have not read it, I encourage you to do so.

From the "order" of the fifties to the "disorder" and eventual "reorder" (ODR) of the sixties, I was on the launch pad by the time I graduated from Bonaventure in June 1968, ready to blast off into adult life. But I'm getting ahead of myself with another significant ODR pattern occurring at the same time, which perhaps best sums up the effects of the sixties on my life and on the lives of many others.

Given the assassinations of JFK, MLK, Malcolm X, and RFK, as well as the many other tragedies, upheavals, and circumstances, ODR was constantly in motion on many levels throughout the country and the world. For me, as previously mentioned, Blessed Sacrament had no demographic diversity and that experience was sustained at McQuaid, where diversity was further diminished since all its students were male. Bonaventure was mostly white, with several Black players on the basketball team comprising most of the school's diversity. I had virtually zero exposure with any BIPOC during those formative years and my family lived happily for the times within the context of whiteness, although we did not perceive it as anything other than natural.

There was no context about "others," despite growing up in the Civil Rights era when the trauma of the Black experience was becoming increasingly publicized throughout the country. I was not engaged or involved at all with this movement, and it is embarrassing to admit that I missed the significance of the whole period, including the summer of 1964's disturbances in the city of Rochester. Most Rochester whites at the time referred to it as the "riots," and still do. But there was a great deal more to the story.

Per Rachel Campbell's story on the Rochester Rebellion on the website BlackPast, the African American population of Rochester grew from 7,845 in 1950 to more than 32,000 in 1964. Much of that population growth came from the South, traveling north in hopes of better socioeconomic conditions. Black migrants were instead met with segregated schools, dilapidated housing, and an unemployment rate more than six times that for whites.

Black residents also suffered from constant public harassment and humiliation, often being referred to as "bean pickers" in a reference to Black migrant workers in the area, as well as being denied housing throughout the city, with African Americans being funneled into the run-down Upper Falls neighborhood. The Rochester race riot also came at a time of especially heightened racial tensions and violence, occurring only a week after a major race riot in Harlem. For more, see https://www.Blackpast.org/african-american-history/rochester-rebellion-july-1964.

Even though we lived less than three miles from where the riots occurred, our more or less "gated" community might as well have been hundreds of miles away. I would read about what was happening in the newspaper, see it on television, or listen on the radio, but do not recall anything being discussed about it as a family. I was not fearful as we went on with our lives. I was about to begin college in just a few short weeks.

My life followed a pattern of detachment with most of the notable national happenings connected with the civil rights movement in the sixties. As I was in high school and then college during this tumultuous period, I could have been more engaged with what was going on in the world, let alone with what was happening a mere three miles away. But that's the way the world worked for many white people. We saw the civil rights movement as not having anything to do with us or our white lives. It was solely a Black problem.

With what I know now, words cannot describe how badly I feel about my lack of awareness, if not indifference. Modern Catholic Church leaders should make note of this and take effective steps to broaden lay awareness and participation. They should also take care and not use the excuse that certain things cannot be discussed because they are "political."

Looking back now, the shallowness of my understanding, knowledge, and interest with respect to consequential issues such as the civil rights movement remains embarrassing and difficult to reconcile. As somewhat described previously, systemic systems

53

within education prevailed and conspired with history and the social norms of the time to provide a time capsule of sheer obliviousness for many whites, including me.

During the early days of COVID in 2020, my wife and I had to cancel a planned civil rights tour experience, including visiting historical places in Montgomery and Birmingham, Alabama. This was to have been a modest attempt to partially reconcile my non-involvement and awareness shortcomings of the past; perhaps now with the pandemic hopefully losing its grip and the availability of vaccines, we can take that trip.

Life was both simple and complex in the post-WWII "Boomer" years of the fifties and sixties. Societal upheaval provided new realities and dramatic change for Catholics, the commonwealth, and the nation in general, yet at the same time still tended to minimize the decades-long struggle over civil and equal rights for all. Thankfully, through the years, important Supreme Court interpretations of the 150-year-old Fourteenth Amendment have helped secure many of these rights in a legal sense. However, there is still a long way to go in blending these legislative steps consistently, effectively, and fully into the normative practices of society.

To get back to ODR sequences or cycles, these were relatively routine, although mostly invisible to me as patterns to understand or be studied. I must say that the "order" stage for me personally probably held from the time I was born well into the sixties. It was not until I was a junior in college that a major personal "'disorder" sequence crept into the picture: the death of my father on Thanksgiving Day, 1966.

Before I get into that life-changing event, a little bit more about Fr. Rohr's philosophy, as it directly relates to my father's passing. Liminality is a word I did not know the meaning of until reading his books and receiving his daily meditations. It is defined as "the quality of ambiguity or disorientation that occurs in the middle stage of a rite of passage, when participants no longer hold their pre-ritual status but have not yet begun the transition to the status they will hold when the rite is complete. During a rite's liminal stage, participants stand at the threshold between their previous way of structuring their identity, time, or community, and a new way, which completing the rite establishes." In other words, it is a term used

54

to identify a person or place considered in-between, or in a state of transition.

Fr. Rohr suggests that the only way out of a person's entrapment in "normalcy, or the way things are," is to be drawn into sacred space, often called liminality, where he believes all genuine transformation occurs. It is an important concept for me because it helps explain how the movement through my own ODR occurs and brings about radical change in the process. For example, my first nineteen years provided the foundation for future change to occur and then, when triggered by disorder circumstances such as the death of my father, provided the opportunity to be transformed to a whole different level of awareness. I leave this topic for now, but ODR patterns will reappear as my story continues.

My father died at the age of fifty-six of a cerebral hemorrhage, leaving a family of six children to the care of my mother. Just two days before the holiday, I had hitchhiked home from college, which he was not too pleased about when he picked me up on the outskirts of Rochester. The next day, Wednesday, my parents went downtown to shop and I tagged along. My father bought me my first suit, which I never forgot as I later found out he couldn't afford it. I went out that night with my brother and a friend and I came back separately with another friend, only to find out that my father was at the hospital just a few doors down the street. I was able to see him, but he died shortly after, and I left my brother and mother at the hospital while I passed on the tragic news to my other siblings.

I was unprepared for such responsibility, and I recall screaming some obscenity into the cold, early morning air that Thanksgiving Day. My sisters and I sat in the kitchen and said some prayers to God, then I had to pull myself together to tell our two younger brothers once they woke up. That's when everything broke down for me. I remember running out of the house, only to be met by one of my father's closest friends who had just arrived.

I was nineteen, my youngest brother was five, and my mother, who was planning on going back to work because of my father's failing funeral business, eventually went back to nursing at Park Avenue Hospital, where coincidentally my father had left this world.

The loss of a parent at such a young age was devastating. Our father was well known and liked, had many friends, and was especially beloved by the nuns at Blessed Sacrament. He was the last of his immediate family, who all died relatively young. Despite being one of the best technical undertakers in the area, his not being a Rochester native was likely a key impediment to developing his business. The demands of his growing family brought him great stress and I'm sure contributed to his untimely death.

As the oldest, even though I was away at college, I tried to help my mother as best as I could. She was remarkable in how she maneuvered through all the details of what was now on her plate. As the sole breadwinner, going back to work for the first time in over twenty years, my mother was faced with raising six kids on her own. Thankfully, the oldest four of us were teens and could help with our two younger brothers.

Over the next three or four years, my mother not only went back to work, but she also leased the funeral home to a new operator, saw me through college, a brother into the Air Force, my sisters through high school, and our younger brothers through grade school. She eventually sold the house on Park Avenue and bought a new home a few miles away on the outskirts of the city. She was simply an amazing woman. The sale of the Park Avenue house was an important step for many reasons, and in hindsight is a revealing experience and an example of how privilege, in my view, worked within our family. As mentioned in the previous chapter, my father bought the funeral home where we lived in late 1946 and took out a twenty-year mortgage for $10,000. As coincidence would have it, the mortgage was paid off in October 1966, approximately one month before he died.

It is important to note that he was the one responsible for this debt and the deed to the property was solely in his name and did not include my mother's name at the time of purchase. Per the records I discovered later, my mother was not a signatory on any of the original 1946 purchase documents.

The reason this is important is that, at the time of my father's death, his funeral home business was bankrupt, and the creditors soon began to circle. Through the assistance of an attorney, somehow my mother's name was officially and conveniently added to the property and her name replaced my father's name on the deed a few weeks after my father died. In a search I did of the county clerk records, I discovered that my father had previously signed over the deed to my mother in February 1965, removing his name, but the transfer paperwork was not officially filed with the clerk until *after* my father's death almost two years later. The result was that this filing saved my mother from losing the house and eventually resulted in sale proceeds in 1969 that otherwise would not have been available to purchase a new family home.

Family lore and other conversations with my mother indicated that her attorney intervened and "took care" of things. A careful examination of the related filed documents at the time are consistent with the interpretation of a late but timely intervention. I am not sure what would have happened if my mother had lost the house due to bankruptcy; other family members no doubt would have helped her.

In terms of actual dollars, from close to zero home equity in 1946, when the initial mortgage was taken out by my father, $20,000 in equity (what my mother sold the house for in 1969) was saved in 1966 through this timely intervention. This then grew to about $50,000 in 1988, which she netted in selling her second house. This money helped to keep the family intact over twenty-plus years. Essentially, my parents' privilege (which to be fair was not that atypical for the times, at least if you knew the right people) paved the way for my mother to be able to raise six children after the loss of her husband. It gives me shudders to think about what could have happened, and that thankfully close friends and relatives were available at the time to assist her.

This is a specific example of how a form of privilege benefited our family. An interesting footnote is that the house my mother sold in 1988 was purchased by a Black couple, so broader access to housing was beginning to open up despite the persistence of redlining.

"White flight" is a close cousin of redlining. The construction of Interstate-490, a major project on the eastside of Rochester, began in the late fifties and was completed in the early sixties. My brother and I used to play home run ball at a park adjacent to the road construction and used the fence as our wall, which we would climb over to retrieve any home run. Thankfully, there was no traffic and probably not too many home runs — at least by me. The new highway would encourage whites to leave the city, as did the white-owned businesses. I saw this firsthand when our family was surprised to learn that a well-known Blessed Sacrament family decided to move to the suburbs, just a few miles away from the city.

Sadly, this was just the beginning of a massive trend that impacted cities throughout the country. The Great Migration of Blacks from the South sparked the white flight and migration into new and fast-growing suburbs via the improved highway systems. I recall driving east on I-490 in the mid-sixties and as I proceeded out, farther and farther, there was hardly any traffic in either direction. It did not take long for this to change with new housing and a megamall built near the also recently constructed thruway, which linked Buffalo to New York City. As the saying goes, "Build it and they will come!"

What whites left behind in many cases were older homes in aging neighborhoods, and redlining practices and de facto segregation policies conspired to herd Black families into the oldest of the old. These days, the reverse is happening with many whites wanting to move back into the city, gentrifying neighborhoods with their newfound wealth through the selling of their suburban properties, therefore forcing Blacks/POC to find other, less attractive housing.

I continued in a somewhat unsettled (disorder) phase after my graduation from Bonaventure and I immersed myself into the role of being the oldest sibling as well as trying to be present for my mother as much as possible. After my father passed away, I occasionally had the thought that the dynamics of my situation as the oldest (a privilege, sometimes) had changed and perhaps some form of relationship shift had occurred within the family.

What I mean by this is that my mother would look to me to be more than just a son but also an advisor, so that my sibling role became blended into a pseudo-father position within the family. It was not always frictionless! My three older siblings were basically more on the scene at home until after I graduated, and my mother's strong character kept us together during these trying times.

With the many prevailing circumstances, plus the winding down of my undergrad experience, I never really had time to grieve my father's passing. It was not until the second semester of my senior year, in a classmate's room, that I finally broke down. I was a residence advisor that year (which thankfully covered my room and board) and I was with a friend who had just dropped out of the Franciscan seminary that year. His sharing the story of losing his father opened me up to tell him about my own loss. I have always remembered that moment, and we became even closer friends. Tragically, he was murdered in Mexico a few years later.

From the time my father died, I was still in "liminal" space and did not move toward the reorder stage until after graduation, when I was hired into a management position and began my career at Rochester Telephone Corp. (RTC). During this time, the overriding sequence and pattern of disorder that dominated the sixties was playing out: JFK, Malcolm X, Vietnam, MLK, protests, and Woodstock. RFK's assassination occurred two days after I graduated and three weeks before I started at RTC.

I had begun a new journey as a freshly minted, college-educated, white male embarking on his professional career and all of this was considered pre-ordained and normal in our white-oriented world. I did not appreciate at all that I was simply the beneficiary of many unearned advantages that I perceived as simply part of the natural order. For example:

• Being recruited by several firms on campus during my senior year

• Being hired into a management position immediately out of college and then placed in an accelerated management development program with at least a dozen or so other males which, although not a guarantee, opened the door to future promotions that did in fact occur

• Securing a hardship deferment from the military draft to assist my widowed mother in her family responsibilities. Because of this I was able to pay off my modest student loan debt within five years of graduation

• Within five years, contrary to many of my classmates and others who had military duty immediately after graduating, I was able to expand my career, develop important professional and social networks, and eventually meet and marry my wife

With these advantages in hand, I offer some "backwards lens" type questions, i.e., what would have happened if:

• I did not go to college?

• I went into the military via ROTC (which was an option at Bonaventure) or the draft?

• My father had lived but continued to struggle with a failing business?

59

- My mother was not able to work?
- Her attorney had not intervened and we lost the house?
- I had been born Black?
- I had been born female?

The answer for each of these: my life would have been drastically different, especially concerning the last two. Since I am neither Black nor female, it is virtually impossible for me to imagine *how* different, but the advantages and privileges that accrued to me automatically from birth as a white male would have been considerably lessened. Let's take them one at a time.

First, if I had not gone to college after graduating from McQuaid it would have been highly unusual. McQuaid was considered a college prep school, and probably less than a handful of my classmates did not move on to the next level (I also would have incurred my father's wrath). But if I did not attend college, since it was the early days of the Vietnam War, a likely scenario would have been that I joined the Navy, like what my brother did by joining the Air Force after he graduated from McQuaid.

If that had been the case, I probably would have gone to college after my military service. This scenario would forward me to 1972-1973 in terms of starting my career, which would have been a completely different situation based on the economic crises occurring at the time. It was therefore highly advantageous that I attended Bonaventure when I did, given all the circumstances that followed, including military deferment.

If I had gone into the military immediately after graduating from college, that would have placed some additional burdens on my mother. I did complete two years of compulsory ROTC training in college but didn't continue after the second year, which was just before my father died. After I graduated, I was not interested in the Army and considered the Navy Supply Corps, given my business degree and the fact that both my parents were ex-Navy. But my brother joined the Air Force, so I got a hardship deferment (a privilege) based on our family situation. Obviously, my professional career would have been delayed had I gone into military service and employment would have presented a different set of challenges four or five years later.

The third question that arises had my father not died in 1966 opens all sorts of possibilities. Even though I was not interested in the funeral business as a profession, I may have opted to help him out on the business side for a time after I graduated. This probably would not have worked because of the low lottery number (58) I had for the draft. So, unless he was somewhat incapacitated and I was able to get a deferment, this would not have worked. Of course, my father still being alive would have allowed for numerous scenarios.

If my mother had not been able to work after my father died, that would have led to several possible scenarios impossible to predict. However, her access into local resources such as family, church friends, contacts with the American Legion, and more would have provided abundant assistance, including jobs for her four oldest children.

Losing our home would been the most devastating, with rippling effects throughout the family for years. Therefore, from a standpoint of privilege — which in this case ascertained that losing the house did not happen — this was significant. My mother would have been forced to find another place to live, perhaps with my two youngest brothers. I was a junior in college and may have had to drop out. My other brother was out of high school, working and eventually joining the Air Force. My two sisters were still in high school but possibly could have lived with other friends or relatives. Life would have gone on somehow, but thankfully "privilege" intervened.

The most noteworthy privilege I experienced other than being white was being male. This allowed me to get a fantastic Jesuit education at McQuaid, be a newspaper boy, get other well-paying, part-time jobs while in high school and college, and after college secure a management position at RTC. It does make me question, though, how my non-white, male brothers and sisters would have fared if they had been similarly advantaged. Opinion: based on what I have observed about Black resiliency and persistence, many would have equaled or surpassed me, but I would say the same of all females, whether Black or white.

If I had been born Black and my father had died prematurely, I think it safe to say the most likely scenario would be that I would have had to drop out of college (if I had been able to afford it in the first place) and either join or get drafted by the Army. From there, based on race and socioeconomic status, who knows?

If I were a white female, I would probably have finished college and then attempt to seek employment in a male-dominated, pre-ERA/Affirmative Action period at a significantly reduced salary than what I started out at. Furthermore, I probably would not have been hired into management, based on the norms of the times, thereby delaying advancement opportunities — if achieved at all. I'll forgo the question of being a Black female as that is getting into complicated space!

The reason for posing these questions is to focus a lens on the nuances of privilege and the resulting benefits that accrued early in my life. Also, it somewhat segues into the next decade and beyond. One caveat: I do not want to simply equate or limit the concept of privilege to material or financial benefits. There are many other important benefits of privilege, such as not being subjected to abuse, mistreatment, injury, or death by law enforcement, not being acknowledged yet closely watched upon entering a store, not being followed on the street because of the clothes you are wearing, and so on. Whites simply do not have to think about these as privileges, yet it is a matter of life and death for Blacks and other POC if they do not!

I close again with a similar question posed in the previous chapter: What words of advice would I give today to my twenty-three-year-old self? Since I more or less "missed" the significance of the civil rights movement, I would encourage this newly minted college graduate to go well beyond his privilege and his book knowledge and, at the start of his career, begin to dig deeper into his worldview.

One way of doing this would be to forge meaningful connections and, as I said before, intentionally seek out wise mentors. At my young age I was living in a super independent manner, not fully understanding what I learned in school, that "no man is an island," to quote John Donne. I truly wish that someone had reminded me of this, but I was lost in my own world at the time and probably would not have accepted the advice. Due to its relevance in my life, I would also suggest that my twenty-three-year-old-self reread *Siddhartha*, but it took a while for the impact of that book to sink in.

Speaking of wise mentors, at my McQuaid graduation party, our next-door neighbor, Jim, gave me some sage advice. He knew how hard I studied in high school and advised me to loosen up a bit in college and take full advantage of the entire experience. Little did I realize what was about to unfold at Bonaventure, and I took his advice to heart, having some of the best years of my life. Since I was the first in the family to ever graduate from college, I lacked someone who might have provided insight into this new stage of my life. Believe it or not, I did not even know the difference between a BBA degree (the program I was in) and a BA degree until my junior year. Tragically Jim died in an apartment fire just a few months later, while I was at school; I have always cherished that special conversation.

Chapter 3
The 1970s: Courage

PIXABAY

Courage over fear.

"A great deal of talent is lost in the world for want of a little courage. *Every day sends to their graves obscure men which timidity prevented from making a first effort; who, if they could have been induced to begin, would in all probability have gone great lengths in the career of fame. The fact is, that to do anything in the world worth doing we must not stand back shivering and thinking of the cold and danger, but jump in and scramble through as well as we can." (Richard Cardinal Cushing on a prayer card, ca. 1970.)*

"One has yet to find very many Catholics, including priests, who are really able to deal with [Blacks] on an equal footing." (Thomas Merton, Seeds of Destruction)

PEOPLE AND EVENTS IN THE NEWS, 1970-1979: Earth Day, Affirmative Action, ERA, Kent State, Watergate, Woodward/Bernstein, Nixon, "Plumbers," Impeachment, Ford, Carter, Vietnam, Berrigans, Jet Hijackings, Oil Crisis, Pentagon Papers/ Ellsberg, Dorothy Day, John and Yoko, Iran Hostage Crisis, Indira Gandhi, Munich Olympics, Bicentennial, "Roots," Wounded Knee, Angela Davis, Apple, Elvis, Pope John Paul II, Three Mile Island, Mother Theresa ... plus, I got married to Sandy and had two children.

When I was into the second draft of this writing, I had a "fear and courage" experience regarding a presentation I was about to make before the Fairport Village Board. It was related to comments made by the Fairport police chief to the Monroe County Legislature about policing in the city, specifically related to two tragic killings of Black males and two other police interactions with children. As I was mentally preparing for what I was going to say that evening, I began to have doubts about whether to proceed, but I did. My comments were less than ten minutes long, but it felt like a lifetime, especially since, per the open forum procedures, there are no comments or questions made by the trustees. This can be intimidating, especially taking a position of "speaking truth to power."

Afterward, the thought popped into my head that, there I was, a white person, speaking to perhaps eight other white people on a Zoom call. How fearful or intimidating would this have been for a Black person? I am grateful I was able to overcome my hesitation (perhaps a prayer I said beforehand helped) and the result was that the mayor contacted me that evening to arrange a follow-up conversation. There is a thin line between fear and courage; however, as I have begun to learn, for a Black person or any BIPOC, that line is solid and often their lives depend on it.

The seventies were transitional years with liminal episodes within several ODR sequences. I was just beginning my professional career, unmarried at the beginning of the decade, and still three years from being ready to settle down. The decade ended being married with a family, the privilege of having purchased two houses, moving back to the neighborhood of my childhood, and in 1979 being at the beginning of what would be a major part of my life's journey i.e., social justice participation and advocacy. The seventies also laid the foundation in the development of important future professional and personal networks that served as the basis for many more new relationships I will discuss later. I cannot say in all honesty that "participation and advocacy" were callings I had, just as I did not envision having a twenty-seven-year RTC career. To a certain extent, that is why courage (as well as its cohort, fear) is the theme of this chapter. I will cite some other illustrations of courage to help underscore the characteristics it takes for one to move through liminality under any circumstances. One of these traits is to develop the confidence that, once order is shaken up and becomes a disordered state, that somehow a new order, or reorder, will take shape and move towards clarity and a new direction. Reflecting on the bookends of this decade, that appears to be what happened in my life and, following the Rohrian model, I attempted to put this direction under the microscope and understand it through the combined pull of courage and fear.

Some impressive "profiles in courage" that occurred during the seventies include baseball great Hank Aaron, in the face of death threats, breaking Babe Ruth's Major League Baseball home run record; Woodward and Bernstein, with their relentless Watergate investigation; and Dorothy Day, with her notable pacifist leadership and imprisonment. In researching these stories, their resolve, persistence, and resilience were inspirational and helped me write this book.

As I humbly attempted to learn from these historical role models, I came to the realization that the courage to take on speaking to the village board was thrust upon me more by circumstance versus anything overtly courageous on my part. Through the combination of strong encouragement from one very supportive friend and then subsequently the Spirit's call, I was inspired and motivated and thus able to discard any underlying fears.

During this writing process, I have noticed how seemingly logical my life's building blocks appear in retrospect. Self-awareness and self-discovery are ever challenging, at least for me, and I am grateful that I can reflect now and see more clearly many of the factors that, unbeknownst at the time, led to dramatic change and opportunity later in my life.

An example of this was moving back to the Park Avenue area and rejoining Blessed Sacrament parish. If Sandy and I had not had the courage to make this move, I am not sure how the following years would have played out. The result was that I have lived almost half of my life in the "Park" city neighborhood, where Blessed Sacrament played a key foundational role in innumerable ways.

As suggested in the previous chapter, the ODR cycle typically starts over and repeats itself quickly and silently, with transparency, although almost by definition under a different set of circumstances.

Such was the case during the seventies, where there were at least two cycles for me. The first (roughly 1970-1973) was the peak of what I labeled as my "five-year plan" after graduating from Bonaventure.

A quick summary: I lived in four different places in the Rochester area, dated several girls, traveled to Europe twice, was promoted to middle management at RTC, continued to be present with the family and helped my mother, was reclassified to 1-A and again became vulnerable to the military draft, paid off my student loans, and met and married my wife, Sandy. To be honest, there were probably two or three ODRs specifically related to privilege within this period.

As I began writing this memoir, it became apparent that "privilege" is a vague and complex topic for white people to understand or interpret. In trying to present the privilege in my own life, I felt it was more a matter of trying to humbly convey an awareness of self-reflection rather than to zealously beat the privilege drum. I did not want to appear that I was in the throes of self-flagellation for having unearned advantages.

Said another way, it is not my intent to overly critique my own sense of privilege, nor criticize others for theirs. I believe it is all in the awareness that whites have many unearned advantages simply based on the color of their skin. But it is what we purposely do with that insight that matters to those less privileged, who ordinarily do not begrudge whites of their privilege; rather, they only want a similar playing field with the same set of rules.

The opportunities presented to me during the seventies are almost too gluttonous to mention, and I simply accepted them with little thought as to the personal advantages that made them possible in the first place. This is somewhat easy for anyone to do, especially for a white male who was able to secure a "hardship" deferment because his father died at an early age, leaving his unemployed wife to raise a family of six. The underpinnings of my rationalization were alive and well and I never once thought that my "hardship" military deferment was based on any unearned advantages (or privileges). This is quite an admission to make, and I accept it completely with insight that now leaves me scratching my head and remorseful while also fully accepting the life contrast it provided versus where (I think) I am right now.

I don't recall being very attached or connected to the post-Vatican II Catholic Church, or even to what Jesus meant in my life. This connection to Church became somewhat more complicated when Sandy and I decided to marry, but eventually worked its way out when she converted to Catholicism. That said, my faith at the time was based more on the traditional religious norms I grew up with rather than anything distinctly spiritual. That would change slowly, and my spiritual journey and relationship with Jesus would require further development over the years within the context of active social justice engagement. Ironically, my involvement with the Church in leadership roles was about to explode by the end of this decade.

Perhaps one small example of my spiritual life relates to the Cardinal Cushing prayer opening this chapter, which was printed on a prayer card I have had for over fifty years. I cannot recall when or where I got the card, and it was kept on various office desks over the years for occasional reference and reflection. Cushing was a courageous person himself, so these words were genuine and authentic to how he lived his life. For instance, he was a member of the NAACP, which was a unique if not surprising affiliation for a high-ranking, white, Catholic prelate. In 1966, Cushing took a courageous position in helping to overturn a ban on the sale of contraceptives in Massachusetts. He clearly was not "stand(ing) back shivering and thinking of the cold and danger."

In this chapter, following the model of Cardinal Cushing, I would like to focus on how else I saw courage personified as I began to discover my own social justice voice. But first, a definition: *courage* is defined in the dictionary as *"having strength in the face of pain or grief."* It is also the ability to act on one's beliefs despite danger or disapproval. Most times, at least in my life and upon reflection, making a choice or taking a position on a topic can be a small, courageous step that then brings forth a torrent of additional steps or choices.

I do not remember why I was drawn to this prayer specifically, but it was at a time when I was stepping out in life during the drama and backdrop of the Vietnam War, where courage was demonstrated daily by our armed forces. I had several friends, classmates, and a relative who served in Vietnam, and a few, sadly, died there. It also took courage to protest this unfortunate and unnecessary war, as some of my other college classmates did as well as national figures such as MLK, the Berrigan brothers, and Jane Fonda. As the headlines and "breaking news" of the times portrayed daily, courage was demonstrated by both military and protest participants.

I was on the front lines of neither but rather a quiet yet interested citizen observer, ambivalent while being caught up in the protests, politics, horrors, and atrocities of a war that seventy-two percent of the country would soon deem immoral. As with the civil rights movement of the sixties, although more self-aware during this period, I did not fully express my social justice voice other than perhaps in discussions with friends or at the ballot box. I was more of a silent observer than an active, courageous participant, but we all must start somewhere.

During these turbulent times, I was fortunate to be beginning my career at RTC, yet another very consequential privilege that opened many doors. From my father trying to inspire me at an early age to become a doctor, lawyer, or perhaps even a funeral director, I had not set my post-college employment sights on working for a highly regulated utility. I started out as a staff accountant and then was quickly selected to the company's accelerated management development program. There were many highs as well as some lows during my telecommunications career, and the company changed drastically during my tenure. The company was led by an aggressive leadership team that acquired several smaller telephone companies all over the country and diversified into lucrative, deregulated markets. I learned a lot, took advantage of the professional opportunities that came my way automatically or that I induced on my own, met hundreds of people inside and outside the company, and have innumerable fond memories of those years.

This was a foundational, professional decade for me in ways I did not fully appreciate until years later. Due to just coming out of college and my relative youth, I struggled early on to understand the demands of the business world. But I was fortunate to have a couple of fantastic mentors who spurred me on — to the extent I was promoted to manager level at the ripe old age of twenty-three. I held several jobs in two different operating departments until taking charge of both the Internal Audit and Corporate Security units in a newly merged position in 1974.

This turned out to be a timely move as, later that year, the company became embroiled in an eight-month-long union strike requiring new security response methods. The audit position also helped shape and sharpen my business and operational skills and the combination of both disciplines provided the opportunity to blend these quite different business units into a high functioning team.

I was also encouraged to engage with their respective professional organizations (the Institute of Internal Auditors and the American Society of Industrial Security) and eventually became president of both local chapters. This is another example of how privilege led to an opportunity to further develop my leadership skills and to be of service to the local community.

These experiences expanded my professional network and brought me into direct contact with the criminal justice community, which provided insights that would be helpful later in my future social justice work. I was also called upon to assist several non-profit organizations such as the United Way, YMCA, George Eastman House, Chamber of Commerce, and the Al Sigl Center.

In the early seventies, RTC, as well as companies throughout the country, were implementing the federally mandated Affirmative Action (AA) program. Oxford Dictionaries defines AA as referring to "a set of policies and practices within a government or organization seeking to increase the representation of particular groups based on their gender, race, creed or nationality in areas in which they were excluded in the past such as education and employment."

RTC had a lot of work to do, especially when it came to hiring more minorities and women into middle and senior level management positions. I was right in the thick of it in the early seventies, working closely with new hires such as an experienced, Black, former county official and a white, female human resources professional, other newly hired, middle management minorities as well as those promoted from within the company.

One thought that parallels the theme of this chapter is that each of these new hires, and those recently promoted, were taking a brave and courageous step in entering a primarily male, white hierarchy. It could not have been easy for any of them, even with the credentials and professional background they brought to the company. Privileges and associated opportunities were opening up and being extended

71

to the 'other' after being long ignored, and even though execution was not perfect in many cases (e.g., effective development and mentoring), it was a beginning through adding diversity in work and life experiences, outlook, and critical thinking.

It was distinctly a win/win for both the company and the new employees, since if you were to be considered a successful and well-run enterprise, staff diversity at all levels was essential. It also discouraged government and other regulators from looking over your shoulder. I was fortunate at such an early stage in my career to be of some assistance at minimum by reaching out to these new management folks, as well as to be able to broaden relationships and in some cases establish friendships.

This turned out to be vital in the coming decades and led me to develop networks I otherwise might not have had. Little did I realize or appreciate at the time that my relationship skills were being developed in ways that would eventually accelerate my future social justice awareness and participation.

Before I move too quickly into that future, I want to pause a bit. As I began writing the second draft of this section, and with the encouragement of a Black friend and female reviewer of the first draft, a few questions were raised. For example, how was I, as a young, college educated, white male, to think that I was suddenly equipped or qualified to professionally interact with POC in a revolutionary new race equity program like AA when I had virtually no exposure to them at any level before?

Being that I was raised in a predominantly white, Catholic environment, this question stopped me in my tracks. The question had never occurred to me. I was not alone, either, since my peers, trainers, and bosses at the time were all in the same boat i.e., white males. Think about that on the flip side if you were a POC. I can see now why this was such an obvious question in her mind, yet I was oblivious.

In responding to her, I described a real story of how I previously attempted to navigate this very complex space. Also, it was happening at a time when I had no realization whatsoever that I was entering a world where I had absolutely no experience or relationships. But, as a rookie manager, I took my AA training into the workplace backed by equally naïve supervisors and AA administrators. Basically, this was the epitome of unadulterated white arrogance fifty years ago. (Could remnants of this attitude still exist today? I'll leave it for each reader to decide).

Around 1972, I was a manager of one of five customer service units at RTC and had an equal number of first line supervisors reporting to me who were responsible for around thirty-five virtually all white, female service representatives. All the supervisors at the time were white females, and when AA was introduced, the demographic mix slowly began to change. A thirty-ish Black female was hired through human resources as a supervisor, and since I had a position available, she joined my team. Having had previous work experience, she was a seasoned professional and, like the other supervisors, did not have any reservations about sharing her thoughts in the office or in team meetings.

Eventually, some disagreements arose between her and another supervisor. The situation appeared to be taking on a personal tone, and I recall having both individual and joint meetings with them to sort matters out and reach some sort of understanding. I cannot recollect how this eventually all worked out, but one of the things I did early on was to invite the new supervisor and her husband out to dinner with Sandy and me. We had a pleasant evening getting to know each other a little better and worked together for a year or two, then I was transferred again due to the development program I was in.

I would not have thought of this experience unless it had been drawn out of me by my friend's question. It struck both of us that, for the times and perhaps even somewhat today, that the dinner invitation step was unusual, especially since I invited them without the benefit of ever having had a previous similar experience. My friend continued to dig deeper into why I did this. All I could come up with is that I took it as a natural course of action for a boss to do, although I admit that most extracurricular meetings with people who worked for me were usually done as a group. Beyond that, I considered it the right thing to do and was likely attracted to the thought that, since I did not have any previous such experience with a Black person, that it was a way to begin and to learn more about my fellow employee as an individual.

This style of supervision and management in valuing the importance of relationships prevailed not just over the duration of my professional career but carried over into my personal life. I consider relationship building to be one of the most important skills I possess, and it has endured prominently in my ongoing social and racial justice journey.

There is another aspect to this story. Typically, for one reason or another and driven by workplace circumstances of the times, my staff teams were predominately female. This segues into another situation that occurred just prior to the one previously recounted.

In 1968, shortly after I was hired at RTC, I was a roaming supervisor learning the ropes in various units in the accounting department before being promoted to manager. Nearly all staff members who reported to me were female. Then I was transferred to another all-female, non-management department supervised by white men. At the time, this "mix" was considered normal in most administrative, non-technical groups and things did not really change until the eighties.

At that time, I again headed up a primarily female unit of business account representatives when the entire telecommunications industry was undergoing fundamental change and increasingly subject to deregulated, competitive challenges. This was leading to several new internal initiatives, which were more or less startups, further complemented by other telecom companies popping up in the marketplace. There was a growing concern among the highly trained staff that they would soon be out of jobs, since it justifiably appeared to them that competition was rapidly beginning to erode the need for traditional RTC products and services.

I called a meeting and suggested that their concerns were probably overestimated since, no matter whether an internal or external startup, these new businesses were going to be looking for people with the exact experience and skills they possessed in abundance. I informed them that I was actively engaged in pursuing internal transfers — and in some cases promotions — which would open doors that, at that point, were very limited. For years I kept a list of those who attended this meeting, and more than half went on to other positions inside and outside the company. The majority of those went on to senior management positions, and in some cases eventually became executives.

To summarize, I consider the advancement of women, not only in this case but others in my career, to be among my proudest accomplishments. But there was another motivation, and that was to

74

help make the organizations they were transferred to or promoted into more professional and efficiently run by these female representatives and their largely unrecognized skills and talents. It was time for women to share in the decades-old privileges heretofore solely intended for mostly white men. I carried this model with me and paid it forward frequently after leaving RTC.

Here is a personal insight about both stories: I can honestly state that my motivations regarding Blacks and women were not driven at all by the demands, policies, and training provided through the implementation of AA programming. The foundational Catholic roots developed through my upbringing and education provided the generosity of spirit that allowed me to be open to others well beyond my deeply imbedded comfort zone as a white male. The seeds of relationship building had already been planted, and these early career and life circumstances nurtured my personal growth and provided the basis for the "tree of Bill Wynne" to grow and flourish even more later in life. And, in a somewhat serendipitous way, they also deepened spiritual growth.

To briefly expand upon this concept, some scriptures with the imagery of a good seedling that grows into a tree come to mind. Later in life, after the cultivation and fertilization of spiritual growth, broad and diverse reading, and use of God given gifts, dialogue with "others" begins to produce enduring fruit. As Jesus said in this parable (Luke 13:6-9):

> There once was a person who had a fig tree planted in his orchard, and when he came in search of fruit on it but found none, he said to the gardener, "For three years now I have come in search of fruit on this fig tree but have found none. [So] cut it down. Why should it exhaust the soil?" He said to him in reply, "Sir, leave it for this year also, and I shall cultivate the ground around it and fertilize it; it may bear fruit in the future. If not, you can cut it down."

Another related quote from spiritual writer W. Philip Keller: "We are identified and known by the sort of fruit, the quantity of fruit, and the quality of fruit borne out in our daily conversation, conduct, and character. There is no greater criterion for Christians." I can only hope that my "tree" flourishes and measures up in this way.

Throughout my career, I was provided the opportunity for not only a steady and upward trending income stream but also the basis for wealth creation. Whenever a new employee started at the company, they were given a small, orange, three-ring binder outlining their present and future benefits, including health care, a pension, and the impact of Social Security contributions at retirement. In 1978, another major benefit was added: a 401(k) plan. Also, my salary and Sandy's income allowed us the opportunity to purchase several houses over the years, building up home equity wealth.

The combination of all these wealth and income factors has now allowed us to live a comfortable retirement and even provided me the time and wherewithal to write this book. The natural forces of privilege converged in my favor, but I also worked hard to make this possible for myself and my family. Yet, in all honesty and humility, I feel I had a head start by being white, and I participated fully in what could be thought of by many as a rigged system that essentially benefits whites more than others.

The question that comes to my mind is how can we, as a society, change the paradigm from privilege for some to rights for all with respect to wealth creation, access to health care, income equality, etc.? For me, there was to be future comeuppance that brought about a major financial setback, but nothing compared to those who do not even have the opportunity in the first place to take a blow and then recoup somehow.

In 1974, Sandy and I purchased our first house on the outskirts of Fairport, had our first child in 1975, and lived there until early 1977, when we decided to move into the city. I had become restless with suburban life and the Park Avenue area was experiencing a resurgence since the time my mother sold the family house in 1969. Sandy, pregnant with our second child, was a bit doubtful about the decision but I was able to convince her it would be a terrific move and, based on the many amazing things and friendships that happened over the following ten years,

I think she would agree that it turned out even better than we could have imagined. This chapter is focused on courage, and it was a courageous step on Sandy's part to leave a comfortable home while pregnant. She had grown up in a rural community and depended completely on my portrayal of the advantages of city life.

Many of our friends and family were surprised by our decision to move back to the city; for me it was more of a calling than a statement. The Park Avenue neighborhood was still very white, but we were markedly closer to energizing diversity compared to the suburbs. The most notable part of the move was re-engaging with the Blessed Sacrament parish community, where so much of my childhood years were attached. It also provided the opportunity for me to better reconnect with the Catholic Church. Sandy also experienced the welcoming parish community and converted not long after we moved. This was yet another courageous decision for her, as she was deeply rooted in her Methodist faith. Her decision provided unity within our family, and I deeply admire her for it.

Even though the Park Avenue area had remained primarily white, it had changed due to economic and social factors as well as the continuing impact of the post-Vatican II era at Blessed Sacrament. "White flight" brought about many demographic changes throughout the neighborhood, including the conversion of a K-8 elementary school at Blessed Sacrament to a junior high school, along with a merger with another nearby parish school. This did not deter us from taking full advantage of what was available for our children, and they were eventually enrolled into this new school system. Through our involvement with the parish, the school, and our city neighborhood, we developed many friendships that have been sustained through the years.

Little did I know, though, how dramatically my life was about to change. I had a small interlude of time in 1977 to reconnect with my roots and share them with my family. We began to participate in the life of the parish and the neighborhood. Having two young children was a magnet for meeting other young families. One thing led to another: I joined the parish choir and Sandy engaged with the church and the neighborhood association.

Her conversion to Catholicism brought her closer to our parish pastor, whom we both knew previously, and that relationship led him to ask me to serve on the parish council. This unleashed the floodgates of almost ten years of active involvement with many programs of the parish and other diocesan agencies and departments. Basically, I became a member of various "tables" which eventually led to many leadership roles. Whether I knew it or not, I was being led by the Spirit in ways I could not have imagined.

In 1979, I was transferred into a sales management position at RTC after five years in an Audit and Security position and, through a friend of mine (the one who introduced Sandy and me seven years earlier), I was nominated to the board of the Catholic Youth Organization. The CYO was affiliated with the Catholic Family Center (CFC), and I only mention this now due to its relevance later.

Unbeknownst to me, I was at the starting gate of my social ministry journey, which is now forty-plus years in the making. It would begin primarily at the governance level (mostly Catholic councils, boards, committees) and would provide the background and connections years later to become more hands-on. Whether I liked it or not, I was being encouraged to share my voice in areas where I had little background at the time.

What words of advice would I give today to my almost thirty-three-year-old self? I would strongly encourage him to carefully consider, critique, and in some cases challenge the promises and influence of authority figures whether in politics, business, church, media, or elsewhere. This would be more with an eye towards the future, but at that young adult age, an appropriate level of discernment should be developed with intentionality. I believe at that time I was simply floating along within life's circumstances and, as I was moving into my many involvements in the eighties, this guidance would have been very important to have had.

Another piece of advice I would give is to take full advantage of the numerous interactions I was having with the Catholic Church to better develop and shape my spirituality. It is very easy to simply declare and demonstrate the outward appearance of faith by getting involved and doing versus the real hard work of being drawn inward and becoming. I believe the former is how I initially started out during the seventies, but this began to change a few years later for many reasons, primarily due to the profound impact of one person I was about to meet.

Chapter 4
The 1980s: Tony

RALPH KOZAK

A painting by Ralph Kozak titled "The Laughing Christ," which was modeled on a sketch, "Christ the Liberator" by Willis Wheatley.

"The greatest challenge of the day is: how to bring about a revolution of the heart, a revolution which has to start with each one of us." (Dorothy Day)

"I have learned that success is to be measured not so much by the position that one has reached in life as by the obstacles which he has overcome while trying to succeed." (Booker T. Washington)

"Today our prime educational objective must be to form men-and-women-for-others; ... men and women completely convinced that love of God which does not issue in justice for others is a farce." (Rev. Pedro Arrupe, S.J., 1973 address; this is still true today)

PEOPLE AND EVENTS IN THE NEWS, 1980-1989: John Lennon, Iran Hostages, Reagan, "Welfare Queens," Atwater, Ollie North/ Iran-Contra, Space Shuttle, Challenger, Black Monday, MLK Day, AIDS, Artificial Heart, Mount St. Helens, Berlin Wall, Gorbachev, CNN, USA Today, "Crack," Ethiopia, Ozone Layer, Fiber Optics, Tiananmen Square, WWW, Lockerbie, Nestlé Boycott, Central Park Five, Lakota Times, Contemplation and Action Center (CAC)

L et me begin with a relevant and embarrassing reflection. I remember distinctly a somewhat well-known, homeless man in his sixties, Dimitri Mamczur, who died tragically underneath a bridge in 1985. His daily meanderings would include appearances all over the city, including the Park Avenue area. At the time, we had only one car and I used to walk to and from my RTC Midtown office location as it was only two or three miles away in city center. Occasionally, I used to see Dimitri walking in the neighborhood but cannot remember ever speaking to him. I am chagrined to admit it, but I likely intentionally avoided him and others like him while on my way to work. It is very easy to be unlike the scriptural Good Samaritan.

In thinking about him now, I feel it was Dimitri and the other homeless on our streets who may have inspired Fr. Tony Valente to open a homeless shelter at Blessed Sacrament. I am so grateful for the gift that both he and Dimitri provided me. Despite my recollection of avoidance on the streets, I was soon able to play a role in providing assistance and support to others in desperate need of shelter. Their combined inspiration provided light and guidance for me and Dimitri's legacy carries on through "Dimitri House," sponsored by Spiritus Christi Church. This program serves those in need by offering a range of programs including food, shelter, and services that help the homeless on their journey toward self-sufficiency.

The eighties contained two major ODR sequences. Within the overall framework of my RTC career, the first half or better of the decade was highly weighted towards volunteer participation in Catholic parishes, agencies, and diocesan life. In the last three years, my volunteer work was greatly reduced for a variety of personal reasons, and I returned to more professional business, educational, and secular pursuits that carried over into the nineties.

80

Most of my volunteer and community work during the first part of the eighties was associated with three Catholic organizations:

- Blessed Sacrament Parish Council – member 1979-1981, one year as president; and a member again in 1985-1987; this also included a great deal of work related to the Joint Parish School Board
- Catholic Youth Organization (CYO)– member of board 1979-1985; President 1984-1985
- Diocesan Social Ministry Board – President 1985-1987

Social ministry is primarily focused on coordinating a call to action to the many social problems that plague the human condition. This call to action consists of two forms: charitable works and social justice. However, many of us tend to confuse works of charity with advocacy and the pursuit of social justice. The United States Catholic Conference of Bishops (USCCB), in its resource entitled "Two Feet of Love in Action," outlines the difference between these two terms:

> Charitable Works are our "response to immediate needs and specific situations: feeding the hungry, clothing the naked, caring for and healing the sick, visiting those in prison, etc." (Deus Caritas Est, no. 31). We step with the Charitable Works foot when we work to aid or assist others both locally and globally to meet their immediate, short-term needs. Examples include engaging in direct service or providing food, clothing, shelter, or monetary assistance to help those in need. "Social justice concerns the social, political, and economic aspects and, above all, the structural dimension of problems and their respective solutions." (Compendium of the Social Doctrine of the Church, no. 201). We step with this foot when we work to address the root causes of problems facing our communities by advocating for just public policies and helping to change the social structures that contribute to suffering and injustice at home and around the world.

My engagement with the Diocesan Social Ministry Board opened my eyes to the many profound issues facing our community and the world yet was focused more on charity work than social justice. My gradual conversion to social justice occurred between

1979 and 1987 and was the period when I truly discovered the "others" around us. This included a deeper appreciation of their needs as well as getting to know many of the people who provided them vital support and assistance, some of whom have continued as friends, mentors, and colleagues to this day. At least one of these friends eventually opened my eyes to go well beyond acts of charity and use my voice for social justice, especially racial justice, and to begin advocating for policy, institutional, and structural change.

As I began thinking about the overall theme and how to structure this chapter, I got stuck. The eighties were significant "breaking out" years for me in terms of social ministry. There was much to write about, but I needed a common thread to stitch together this part of my story. One night, when I was trying to sleep, it came to me: Fr. Anthony Valente, or whom Sandy and I know simply as "Tony."

As coincidence (or perhaps not!) would have it, I would occasionally see this gangly, dark haired, forty-ish guy at the Downtown YMCA where I worked out, not knowing that he was a diocesan priest. Things changed dramatically in August 1980, when he walked into Blessed Sacrament as the newly appointed pastor, just after I was elected Parish Council President. We struck up an immediate friendship and, due to his more hands-on program orientation and persona versus anything administratively oriented, he relied on me frequently.

Blessed Sacrament parish was quickly developing demographically into a complex melting pot (but still very white) as a result of geography and the increasing "white flight" from the city to the newly developing suburbs. This included many of the people and families I knew growing up, with large, single-family homes now being broken up into apartments. The younger people and families now moving into the parish ranged politically from far right to far left.

Tony was distinctly well left of center, based on his upbringing, priestly experience, and most importantly due to his genuine interest and concerns for those who were marginalized and less privileged. I was more of a moderate but would usually steer left on social justice issues, so we were usually on the same page. Tony had a hearty laugh and was deeply spiritual, relational, charming, humble, and charismatic. Our friendship grew and he literally became part of our family, as will be seen later. He not only became one of my best friends but also an older brother I never had.

Within a year or so of becoming pastor, Tony brought in the well-known and controversial Fr. Philip Berrigan to make a presentation in the church. Together with his brother, Daniel, also a Jesuit priest, they led the antiwar and antidraft movements during the Vietnam War. Philip served in the US Army in World War II, becoming a priest in 1955. Daniel, an intellectual and theologian ordained in 1952, complemented his brother's activism. The church was filled both inside with listeners and outside with protesters, many of whom were my friends asking me how, as Parish Council president, I could have allowed this to happen.

Needless to say, Tony made parish life interesting. He consistently pushed the envelope by promoting a social justice agenda. His exuberance became especially apparent when he led the move to establish an overnight homeless shelter in the church basement for the least of our brothers and sisters.

Shortly after my term on Parish Council, Tony asked me to attend an upcoming meeting in the rectory regarding the establishment of the overnight shelter. About thirty people were crammed into the living room, trying to organize for this important new ministry, and Tony was no help. Anxious to formulate a plan of action, I drew up a basic matrix by date and hours of operation for people to simply sign up for a time. This step jump-started the launch of the shelter within a week. I can still remember driving home after the meeting and suddenly turning around because I had overlooked signing up myself! This was to be one of the first, if not the first such homeless shelter in the diocese and preceded Sr. Grace Miller's "House of Mercy" shelter by a year or two. Despite its immediate success, it faced controversy as some parishioners deemed it inappropriate for the shelter to be in the church and thought it a liability for the parish.

Tony was unfazed and, as it turned out, Sandy was the victim of just one of the few serious incidents that occurred. One of the overnight guests pulled a knife on her. But in a timely act of intervention, one of the supervisors was able to talk the person through it and defuse the situation with no physical harm done. I was not aware of the incident until after Sandy returned home, and I was proud of how calm she was and of the peaceful outcome.

The ministry continued for several years and eventually morphed into the Blessed Sacrament Soup Supper program, which has been in existence since the early nineties. My life was markedly enriched by having been a part of this ministry, and our friendship with Tony deepened even more. Sandy and I went from coordinating parish parties at the nationally renowned Oak Hill Country Club to participating in the creation and operation of a homeless shelter through Tony's gentle and fearless inspiration.

In 1983, Tony moved on to another assignment, but we continued to see each other regularly. He became a close confidant, mentor, and advisor for my growing involvement with social ministry in the diocese. He had many connections with people involved in that important work. Additionally, my involvement on the CYO Board, specifically the last two years when I was president, brought me into direct contact with many high-level diocesan social ministry leaders. In January 1984, the bishop chartered a process for the Renewal of Social Ministry to realign the dozens of agencies in the diocese with scores of diverse programs and funding streams into a more organized, cohesive framework. Together with CYO's executive director, we were the representatives in this process.

Our efforts were apparently highly regarded, and the team leadership recommended to the bishop that I be appointed as the chairperson of the newly formed Diocesan Board of Social Ministry, which took effect in July 1985. This began a two-year journey of leadership, discovery, learning, execution, and implementation involving all facets of diocesan social ministry.

There were some discoveries as to how the bureaucracy of the Church operated through this appointment, at least in my view. As mentioned previously, I was involved with the renewal process through my role as president of the CYO board. CYO was basically a gnat in size and significance given the array of agencies and organizations affiliated with diocesan social ministry. Despite our size, we were one of the most vocal, particularly as it related to continuity of funding streams. Suffice it to say that our input was not always appreciated, so we were very surprised when the bishop asked me to consider being the first chairperson, effectively leading the fulfillment of the entire renewal process.

The CYO board and I then had to decide about whether to sustain our challenging of material financial matters versus possibly playing a key role in influencing the implementation agenda. We chose the latter, and this was another learning experience that would be of great value through the years when dealing with Church hierarchy.

I also met and worked with several people during this period who would continue to be special influences for me over the following decades. They include Joyce Strazzabosco (CYO executive director), Gaynelle Wethers (CYO board member and a future chairperson of the Diocesan Board of Social Ministry), and Marv Mich, who moved into Blessed Sacrament during this period and eventually became the Director of Advocacy and Parish Social Ministry at Catholic Family Center. He was the author of several books and articles on Catholic social teaching and interfaith dialogue. He passed away in 2019.

Getting back to Tony, how do I begin to assess the impact he had on my life — and perhaps mine on his — in connection with social justice during his time at Blessed Sacrament and beyond? As I look back, Tony exemplified justice through the legacy of his works, such as establishing one of the first homeless shelters in the diocese. The sense of justice he manifested through his saintly presence, openness, and authentic listening ability shined brightly for all to see. His approachable, peaceful demeanor became the shoulder people could cry on.

For me, he was like a flashlight illuminating my path of social justice. Given my Franciscan education, I likened him in mind and spirit to many Franciscans I had known. Among his priest colleagues, he was considered a "priest's priest" (a direct quote from a fellow priest at Tony's funeral in 1995, after he passed away tragically at the age of sixty-one). I take that description to mean that Tony was a special servant who stood unique among his peers. As the diocesan bishop, Mathew Clark, said in a tribute, "Tony put a human face on the kindness of Christ for all he served during his thirty-six years of priestly ministry."

Sandy and I were blessed and honored by Tony allowing us to enter his life. This is best exemplified when, at Easter in 1984, he gave us a print of "Christ the Liberator," otherwise known as the "Laughing Christ" (see the picture at the beginning of this chapter).

We had never seen this portrayal of Jesus before, and on the back of the picture was this inscription:

"To Bill & Sandy –This is a print of Christ the Liberator. I give this special print to you because you often helped to set us free."

No matter where we have lived, this picture has always been in a prominent focal point of our home, and each time I look at it I cannot help thinking of a laughing Tony as the personification of the "Liberator." Even if he were not the one who gave us this picture, and we asked ourselves who came to mind, the answer would be "Tony." I would be hard pressed to explain why Tony identified Sandy and me with "Christ the Liberator," but I think we were both receptive to the work that our friend was trying to do at Blessed Sacrament and his message of social justice. Sandy and I were among his strongest advocates in a parish that had both far right and far left views among the laity. We counted members of all persuasions among our friends, so perhaps Tony saw us as helpful ambassadors.

Another interesting question posed to me by my inquisitive Black reviewer was, "Is your journey not only seeking liberation for the 'other' and to help set them free but also seeking liberation for yourself and setting yourself free?" I must admit the question is deep and complex. I could attempt to answer with a simple "Yes," but, upon some prayerful reflection, what I would mean by my affirmative answer is that, as my life has been enriched over the past several years on this social and racial justice journey, I have been liberated from the self-imposed shackles of fear and silence to find my path and voice.

To this day, I am still overwhelmed by the words Tony shared on that print. When he gave it to us, we had known him less than four years. His impact on our lives was immediate and overwhelming. In writing this memoir, I was challenged to dig deeper, beyond the few examples I provided previously in my work with Tony. I know that we are not alone in stories of his graciousness and gratitude, but what other messages was he giving us with that print and that powerful inscription?

Out of many possibilities, I have come up with one: just like Tony lived his life and Jesus his, that he was suggesting that we are to continue to pay it forward. "It" in this case would be to continue our journey of seeking liberation for the "other" and to help set them free. I must be honest and say that, in 1984, the print was merely accepted as a gift without consideration of any future implications. For Tony, it was a recognition, but I also suspect that he was challenging us to sustain our social justice journeys, and when I gaze at "Christ the Liberator," I continue to see his light today, illuminating my path.

Tony apparently saw something in me back when I was thirty-seven years old; it has taken an equal amount of time since to figure out the deeper meaning in my life as it has continued to unfold. In the eighties, I was focused on using my abilities that were developed during my education at Blessed Sacrament, then nurtured further at McQuaid and St. Bonaventure. I had served all four of the Blessed Sacrament pastors since its founding and was about to be asked to serve the fifth. I had also been called to do the same in other diocesan capacities.

I am forever grateful for Tony's awareness of whatever gifts of mine he saw at the time, but more importantly the challenge he presented to live more fully over the years. To say something as he did to Sandy and me is truly humbling and, somewhat unwittingly, has directed my path. You may want to ask yourself, "Who are the people who have helped me in my life, similar to how Tony impacted Bill's and Sandy's, and how have they guided my way?"

In 1984, I was honored by the Catholic Charities Board of Trustees when the bishop presented me with their St. Vincent DePaul Award. Tony also attended. It read, "For (your) Many Contributions to the Growth and Development of the Catholic Charities Movement in the Diocese of Rochester." This recognition no doubt contributed to my selection as the first chairperson of the Diocesan Social Ministry Board the following year, and I believe was also given for my work at the parish level, together with my good friend Tony at my side.

In the early eighties, another program Sandy and I engaged in as a couple at Blessed Sacrament was high school youth religious education, including facilitating youth retreats and in-home Masses. We were also selected to be presenters as a couple for the Sacrificial Giving Program, which led to being loaned out several times over the years to other parishes for presentations. Additionally, we took time to do a couples retreat through the well-known "Marriage

Encounter" program and were fans of the author of *Living, Loving, and Learning*, Leo Buscaglia. Looking back, I find it hard to believe how we found the time to do all we did. But then I remember that we had the inspirational and charming Tony.

I also had a somewhat humbling learning experience when I was the Parish Council president during Tony's tenure. I took on the task to update the council bylaws as they were out of date after ten or so years. An energetic, eighty-ish, former teacher who was on the council would not deviate one iota from insisting that her Seniors committee maintain full status, as opposed to being a sub-committee, which was my recommendation. Meeting after meeting, we went through the council approval process and made changes, but she would not budge on her position, and no one wanted to challenge her. It got to be somewhat humorous after a while (at least to other council members) and I finally relented. There were several lessons learned with this experience but swallowing my pride of authorship and deferring to maturity and wisdom was the most significant.

After Tony left Blessed Sacrament, I remained involved with parish work and was again called upon by our new pastor, Fr. Bruce Ammering, to serve another term on the Parish Council. During this period, I became more closely involved with the Joint Parish School Board and educational diocesan leadership, primarily regarding assessing other possible school consolidations. This led to a disheartening event which forced Blessed Sacrament's junior high to close its doors permanently. The relentless demographic changes attributed mainly to white flight were ravaging urban parishes as the suburban Catholic schools continued to grow. It was only a matter of time before things began to change for those in the suburban schools as well.

In 1988, a nearby suburban parish was chosen to establish a Catholic junior high school less than two miles from Blessed Sacrament's school. The bishop's decision came out of the blue, since Blessed Sacrament had been involved in the discussion process together with several other urban (said another way, "under stress financially and diversified") parishes. They were to evaluate, determine, and recommend a comprehensive consolidation plan to the bishop.

The backdrop was that several nearby suburban (said another

way, "wealthy and virtually all-white") parishes with schools banded together and apparently convinced the bishop to establish a new suburban Catholic junior high school. From what I recall, there was a concern among the suburban Catholic schools and parents that their kids might be forced to go to schools in the city. I wrote the bishop in protest, but I do not recall if he ever responded.

This action was the death knell of Blessed Sacrament Junior High and would result in a perfectly usable facility designed for a K-8 school system being left vacant. Our daughter was in the eighth grade at the time, and as irony would have it, I was asked to deliver the last commencement speech to graduating eighth graders in 1989. I leave it to the reader to discern whether there was classism or racism involved, but at best it smacked of a form of anti-urban/city bias.

And as history has demonstrated, over the next thirty-plus years, Catholic elementary parish schools have now virtually ceased to exist in the diocese. The next step in consolidations and closures began to focus on entire Catholic parishes and their churches (In a later chapter, there is a more modern example regarding an historic church in a Latinx community). An interesting factoid about the status of the Blessed Sacrament school: it is now the home of an organization called "Refugees Helping Refugees" and is a resource for Sandy in her work with a refugee family.

To be fair, there are at least three major issues at play here, not only with the Diocese of Rochester but dioceses throughout the country e.g., the declining number of priests and religious, dramatic decreases in Mass attendance, and the subsequent financial devastation that occurs as a result. However, I would suggest, based on my own personal involvement and observations over the years, that what is seriously lacking in these conversations and processes is a clear, transparent diocesan vision and an overall strategy that is more community-focused.

Regarding my extended family, in the late seventies and early eighties I was researching our family genealogy after watching the famous "Roots" series, which told the story of a fictional character (Kunta Kinte). The TV production was based on one of author Alex Haley's ancestors, a Gambian man born in 1750, enslaved and taken to America where he died in 1822. My interest was spurred to explore my own roots and, to make a long story short, led me to coordinate two family reunions on my mother's German side within a seven-year period.

Over the years since, I have utilized a couple of DNA ancestry-related data bases to develop a family tree of well over 500 names. Nearly all of Sandy's and my lineage is Western European-based, with no surprising revelations such as those discoveries made by Henry Louis Gates Jr. involving celebrity guests on his "Finding Your Roots" show.

Gates was interviewed for AARP magazine in 2020: "The overall message of 'Finding Your Roots' is that we're a nation of immigrants. Even Native Americans migrated here 16,000 years ago across the Bering Strait. African Americans were unwilling immigrants who came here in chains. But now with DNA we can tell the multiplicity of places that their ancestors came from, including the fact that the average African American is 24 percent white or European and one-third of all African American men are descended from a white man, like I am. There is no racial purity. At the level of genome, we are 99.9 percent the same."

When one thinks about Gates' words with respect to the racial injustice that continues to endure in this country after over 400 years, one must ask, "Why?"

At a family gathering in the late eighties, I recall a conversation where I casually suggested that Oliver North should have gone to prison due to his many crimes involving the Iran-Contra affair (North is an American political commentator, television host, military historian, author, and retired Marine Corps lieutenant colonel. He eventually was jailed but legal battles ensued, and all charges were eventually dropped a few years later).

The family discussion turned into an animated conversation and, for the most part, anything deemed "political" was avoided at future gatherings. This established a pattern of what I would call an unhealthy silence and avoidance of significant topics of the day. As long as the conversation is light, airy, or superficial, all is well. It took me many more years to figure out that, even though our DNA is similar, mine is not wired the same way when it comes to being silent!

In 1987, I was selected by RTC to pursue an MBA at the University of Rochester's Simon School of Business. Due to the two years required for this program and other work demands, I pulled back from nearly all my church and community work. To be honest, after seven years of toiling in "church vineyards," it was time to pull back and recharge a bit. Also, after ten years of city life, Sandy and I decided to experience building a house, so we moved back into the suburbs. Our two oldest children would soon be heading into high school and Blessed Sacrament Junior High was closing. The "tea leaves" were suggesting a change.

As it turned out, this was just the beginning of several momentous events within a brief period. Shortly after getting my MBA in 1989, we had our third child (Tony is his godfather) and then, within eight months of that, I had a work-related transfer out of Rochester to RTC's downstate telephone company properties just outside of New York City. This led to building yet another house within three years, another ODR cycle or two, and a complete upheaval of life as we had known it.

And so, what words of advice would I give today to my almost forty-three-year-old self at the conclusion of the eighties? The inherent dangers, traps, and attraction of ego (or the "false self," as Rohr would describe it) is something I would point out to myself. During the eighties, I was being called upon and recognized in many ways, and it was very compelling to begin to swim in my own "juice." One can begin to think very highly of himself due to special work assignments and promotions, community recognition, and calls from the bishop.

I would advise myself today to not get caught up in the prestige of involvements with boards, committees, and the like but to also be participative and hands-on with the people and communities I was purportedly serving. I did not really do this with conscious intentionality for another twenty years or so.

With that advice in mind, it is fitting that I conclude this chapter with a last reflection about Tony, namely, that his light was revealed to me through the natural and authentic way he conducted his life and furthered the causes of the marginalized in our midst.

One final note: the last item in my list of eighties events is the Center for Action and Contemplation (CAC), established in 1987 by Fr. Richard Rohr, OFM. I will have more to say later about his significant impact on my life.

Chapter 5
The 1990s: Separation and Renewal

PEXELS

The Roseman Covered Bridge, Winterset, Iowa, featured in the novel *The Bridges of Madison County.*

"When you part from your friend, you grieve not; For that which you love most in him may be clearer in his absence, as the mountain to the climber is clearer from the plain." (Khalil Gibran, The Prophet)

"There is cause to be thankful even for rebellion. It is an impressive teacher, though a stern and terrible one ... The thing worse than rebellion is the thing that causes rebellion." (Frederick Douglass, December 1866, The Atlantic)

"In simple terms, I would say that the message is this: white society has sinned in many ways. It has betrayed Christ by its injustices to races it considered "inferior" and to countries which it colonized. In particular, it has sinned against Christ in its lamentable injustices and cruelties to [Blacks]. The time has come when both white and [Black] have been granted, by God, a unique and momentous opportunity to repair this injustice and to reestablish the violated moral and social order on a new plane." (Thomas Merton, Seeds of Destruction)

PEOPLE AND EVENTS IN THE NEWS, 1990-1999: Rodney King, LA Riots, O.J., Clinton, Lewinsky, Impeachment, Windows 95, Dial-up, Netscape, Seinfeld, Hummer, Princess Di, Hubble, Desert Storm, Mandela, Waco, Euro, World Trade Center, Oklahoma City, Columbine, Yugoslavia, Gulf War, Rwanda, The Troubles, NAFTA, Hurricane Andrew, Chunnel, human genome, Anita Hill, Mother Theresa

Despite my Catholic upbringing and my multi-level engagement in church organizations over the years, the early nineties provided an opportunity for some introspection in answering the question, "What next?" — especially since I was about to be physically separated from my Rochester experiences. Churchwise, these roots were framed more religiously than what I would call spiritually, and more governance-oriented than directly participative with the marginalized.

Essentially, my Church experiences up to this time were cast more in its traditional, authoritarian, and hierarchical mode i.e., pre-Vatican II, Ten Commandments, Baltimore Catechism. Then, after Vatican II opened the Church's windows into the modern world, it became more socially responsible, updated its liturgy, gave a larger role to laypeople, opened more dialogue with other religions, and much more. Even though I participated in Church matters in the early days of post-Vatican II and fully endorsed its changes, it began a decades-long process of not only learning but un-learning.

The decade was very different personally than the previous one, and a couple of extreme ODR sequences brought this about. The most traumatic experience was the 1990 uprooting of my family due to a job transfer downstate, fifty miles or so outside of New York City. This was the first time I had lived outside of Rochester, other than my college experience at Bonaventure near the small city of Olean, which was somewhat in the shadow of Rochester.

However, it was easier for me to adapt than for Sandy and our two oldest (Allyson and Sean) as I had the continuity of being connected within the RTC family and already knew people at my new work location. In a pre-Internet, social media-cell phone-oriented world, the family became virtually cutoff from relatives, friends, doctors, schools, and basically all things familiar.

94

Our reorientation was further impacted by building a second house while our youngest (Andrew) was less than a year old. I thought the title of this chapter fitting, especially as there was an identical and reverse sequence that occurred just five years later.

We lived in the small town of Goshen and became somewhat of a fixture in the community. I joined the Rotary Club and was appointed to the foundation board of the local hospital, serving as its treasurer, and Sandy was an active member of its auxiliary. These each provided many social opportunities, and it was a different life than our Rochester experience. We were living and being active in a much smaller "pond."

Likewise, Allyson and Sean were both involved with their schools, and eventually Andrew entered pre-school, so these provided connecting possibilities for Sandy and me as well. The new dimensions of our world provided a stark contrast to our previous life. Moreover, we were in the shadow of The Big Apple and all it had to offer.

Being on the doorstep of the melting pot of New York City presented a dichotomy in that the downstate Goshen area where we lived was predominantly white. The employees I worked with, our neighborhood, the Rotary I belonged to, the Foundation Board I was a member of, and the church we belonged to were a vast sea of whiteness, yet an hour car trip away was a city teeming with unimaginable diversity (An interesting side note: the Hasidic village of Kyrias Joel was in the town of Monroe, near my place of employment. This unique, all-white community has a population today of over 25,000, having one of the youngest median age populations of any municipality in the United States as well as one of the highest poverty rates).

As I mentioned, we were also members of the local Catholic parish but were not nearly as involved as we had been at Blessed Sacrament. However, we were soon confronted with a situation of clergy sex abuse at our new parish. This preceded by at least a decade or so what we know today as the plague of sexual abuse within the Church. A few years later, after we returned to Rochester, we eventually joined a somewhat controversial, urban, Catholic parish with the ironic name of Corpus Christi, or "Body of Christ." I say that as the name assumes not just the literal human body of Christ, but also the meaning of "body" as inclusive of all people.

The irony is that the Corpus Christi community was forced to shut down due to encouraging Eucharistic participation with non-Catholics, a broader liturgical role for women, and active ministry with the LGBQ+ community. The combination of both parish experiences in Goshen and Rochester would become important years later, when I continued to be confronted with my increasing spiritual curiosity about the role and purpose of the Church and where I fit in, if at all.

The "through line" of my personal social and racial justice journey was somewhat suspended during the early nineties and followed a dynamic, experiential, and secular script, similar to the early seventies. I was the lead management person on three separate labor negotiations that concluded favorably and without incident for both the unions and management. We went to the city for shows, dinners, and shopping almost monthly. Sandy and I even traveled to Ireland, which was her first time in Europe. I was able to meet some of my Irish family for the first time.

On a broader, national level, two historical racial justice events happened in the early nineties that directly relate to the objectives of this memoir. The first happened shortly after we moved to our new home in Goshen and involved the brutal police beating of Rodney King and subsequent trial that resulted in devastating riots. According to news reports, King was beaten by LAPD officers after a high-speed chase during his arrest on March 3, 1991, for drunk driving. An uninvolved individual filmed the incident from his nearby balcony and sent the footage to a local news station. The footage showed an unarmed King on the ground being beaten with clubs and kicks after initially evading arrest. The incident was covered by news media around the world and caused a public furor.

Four officers were tried on charges of use of excessive force. Of these, three were acquitted, and the jury failed to reach a verdict on one charge for the fourth. Within hours of the acquittals, riots started, sparked by outrage among racial minorities over the trial's verdict and related, longstanding social issues. The rioting lasted six days and 63 people were killed, with 2,383 more injured; it ended only after the California Army National Guard, the United States Army, and the United States Marine Corps provided reinforcements. The federal government prosecuted a separate civil rights case, obtaining grand jury indictments of the four officers for violations of

King's civil rights. That trial ended with two officers being found guilty and sentenced to serve prison terms. The other two were acquitted. In a separate civil lawsuit, a jury found the city of Los Angeles liable and awarded King $3.8 million in damages.

Due to the incident's national notoriety, to this day the name Rodney King conjures immediate recollection of the brutal police beating of a young Black man, much like George Floyd's name evokes today. What is not so clear to me is what I felt about King then, in contrast to where I am today regarding racial justice advocacy. What I can say is that I was clueless about the relationship of the Rodney King matter to an even more famous incident that happened in LA just a few short years later: the O.J. Simpson case. I do not think I have to go into detail about the O.J. case. I, as well as most whites, was more than a little incredulous about the "not guilty" verdict after the most observed trial in history.

Within my white mindset, I made no connection to the Rodney King incident at all. What I am referring to is that, even though the police assault on King happened four years before the Simpson case, the racial tensions and mistrust of the LAPD by Blacks and minorities in general had never changed and continued to fester. White people were largely oblivious to any association with previous racial injustices and merely thinking of the inevitably of a guilty verdict. I know I was.

I can still recall where I was and whom I was with when the police were chasing O.J.'s white Bronco, as well as when the verdict was read. There was absolutely no doubt in my mind of his guilt and like many others I was stunned. The point I want to make is not whether he was guilty or innocent, but the sense of justice that was overwhelmingly felt by the Black community: a day of reckoning had finally come to the white-dominated criminal justice system. The "not guilty" verdict provided many Blacks with some vindication and payback for the injustices inflicted on them for two centuries.

Right or wrong, it was celebrated throughout the Black community, in stark contrast to the rioting that occurred after the King verdict. This begs another question: are protesting and rioting worse than the incidents which incited the protests/riots in the first place? This is a problem that still dominates racial justice discussions today, an example of which is the 2020 George Floyd police killing in Minneapolis. Even Frederick Douglass reflected on this conundrum almost 160 years ago.

A friend, mentor, and colleague of mine, Frank Staropoli, writes the blog "A White Guy in Rochester" and had this to say in a September 2020 post:

"For People of Color, we are the British – times some multiplier. Over 400 years we have overseen a society that dominates Black people. And each time we seemed to correct that original sin of enslavement, we conjured up a more devious way to maintain dominance: sharecropping, Jim Crow, lynching, mass incarceration. And despite the marginal advances of the Civil Rights era, through several iterations, we've constructed and upheld a network of systems and institutions that continue not only to disadvantage Black people, but to imprison and to kill them in outrageously disproportionate numbers.

"We are the primary beneficiaries of the violence used to establish our nation. If our predecessors resorted to extreme violence over high taxes and the right to own human beings, who are we to criticize the methods of uprising by those on whose necks we have knelt for centuries? How do we dare criticize the tossing of a few bottles or rocks or fireworks, or the breaking of a couple of dishes and glasses? How blind and ignorant can we be not to see past the few desperate incidents of violence and hear the cause of the protest?"

During our Revolutionary War era, even John Adams once said, in reference to the colonists' treatment by the British, "We won't be their Negroes."[6] His words are ironic and startling in the context of current events. Would we call or otherwise label Revolutionary War heroes at the mistitled Boston Tea Party as "looters," "thugs," or in today's terms "un-American?" There is a lot to unpack here, especially for whites reading this who are bestowed great privilege, including that of being unwilling to even examine how our roots as a country are premised on protests and riots and not something so wrongly labeled in history as a "party!"

The story of my gradual justice awakening comes a couple of chapters from now, but my view was clouded by my white perception of justice and how it works. I thought O.J. got off because of his celebrity, his money, and his access to a "dream team" of celebrated attorneys as well as other criminal defense professionals. This is just part of the story, as well as the "reasonable doubt" carefully introduced by O.J.'s defense team. Bottom line: our white privilege-dominated society was completely blindsided by the verdict.

Another real-world illustration that dramatically exposes white privilege is contained in a *New York Times* feature story from December 2020, about a Black male teenager from Virginia whose mother is Black and his father white. To quote directly from the article, "Shortly after his 18th birthday in July, Mr. Galligan asked his father, a former law enforcement officer, what he thought about white privilege. 'The first thing he said to me is that it doesn't exist,' Mr. Galligan recalled. He then asked his father if he had ever been scared while walking at night, or while reaching into the glove box after getting pulled over by the police. He said his father had not. 'That is your white privilege' Mr. Galligan said he told him. For every Black person in this country this example of a privilege they do not have is something they face and endure every day."

I present this excerpt to illustrate my personal obliviousness as it demonstrates how white privilege works to disconnect whites from realities that they are not conditioned to see or even consider. This applies at several different levels. First, even though O.J. is Black and would typically be more than suspect given the details of the murders, many were inclined to give him a break initially given his notoriety and fame as one of the most famous football players ever, a sports announcer, and a movie star. He was extremely well known, admired, good looking, and rich. He was treated with kid gloves (ignore the pun!) though being charged with the gruesome murders of his wife, Nicole Brown Simpson, and Ronald Goldman changed his image. Rodney King had none of these advantages when he was brutally attacked. Yet, it was easy to ignore or downplay King's case if you were white — until the riots made that impossible.

I simply conclude this discussion by admitting I am once again embarrassed that I missed any connection between these two historical, relatively adjacent moments in race relations but now understand how it happened; at some point, clarity and a deeper remembrance entered in, but it took years for the fuller awareness associated with being a part of the white, dominant culture to present itself.

Beyond this background and with deeper reflection, the Rodney King beating, the subsequent police acquittal, and the O.J. verdict suggest to me that the persistent endurance of police brutality on Blacks almost thirty years later informs, confirms, and energizes my continued advocacy for racial justice. At the time, and like some of the characters in the parable of the Good Samaritan, I was merely an observer and bystander. This demonstrates how deeply imbedded the roots of white supremacy are within me, as well as the ruling class of white society. This is especially true within the entire criminal justice system.

There was another story that dominated the news in 1993 to which I did have some direct exposure, but again demonstrates how I missed the significance. In my move downstate with RTC, I was now working as a member of the senior team in a subsidiary that included telephone companies that RTC had acquired across the country. There would be convenings and meetings in out-of-state locations, and one of these was held at a company headquartered in Monroeville, Alabama, birthplace of Harper Lee, author of *To Kill a Mockingbird*.

As circumstance would have it, just before my visit that year and per a March 1993 *New York Times* article, a Black man named Walter McMillian walked out of a Bay Minette, Alabama, courtroom a free man after prosecutors conceded that he had spent six years on Alabama's Death Row because of perjured testimony and evidence withheld from his lawyers. The story said:

> Whether he was also put there for being a Black man who violated the racial and sexual taboos of the small-town South is only one of the issues swirling around a case that has evoked far broader questions of race and justice.
>
> Almost everything about Mr. McMillian's conviction in 1988 for the shooting death of an 18-year-old white female store clerk now seems extraordinary. From the start, the case was enveloped in a volatile mixture of race and sex stemming from Mr. McMillian's involvement with a white woman. Mr. McMillian, who is 46 years old, was locked up on Death Row even before he was tried. The state built a case on suspect testimony and withheld crucial evidence that called that testimony into question.
>
> In the end, it was a decision by the trial judge to treat Mr.

McMillian as harshly as possible that allowed Mr. McMillian to win his freedom. If the jury's sentence of life in prison without parole had been left in place, Mr. McMillian might have been another forgotten Black inmate in an Alabama prison. But the judge overruled the jury and condemned Mr. McMillian to die in the electric chair. Because of the death sentence, Mr. McMillian's case was vigorously appealed, and eventually overturned. To many of his defenders, Mr. McMillian's conviction for the killing seemed like an updated version of the book *To Kill a Mockingbird*, in which a Black man was falsely accused of raping a white woman.

An interesting footnote to this story is that McMillian's attorney was Bryan Stevenson, who currently runs the Equal Justice Initiative (EJI) located in Montgomery, Alabama, and is the author of the book *Just Mercy*, which was made into a movie a few years ago. EJI provides legal representation to prisoners who may have been wrongly convicted of crimes, poor prisoners without effective representation, and others who may have been denied a fair trial. Stevenson's organization never lacks for work and has been tremendously successful in overturning cases such as McMillian's.

What personally disturbs me about these three stories is that the light and example that Fr. Tony provided me just a few years before had not taken root. The recounting of them demonstrates that I still had the "plank" (and still have, occasionally) in my own eye as quoted from Luke 6:41-42:

> Why do you look at the speck of sawdust in your brother's eye and pay no attention to the plank in your own eye? How can you say to your brother, "Brother, let me take the speck out of your eye," when you yourself fail to see the plank in your own eye? You hypocrite, first take the plank out of your eye, and then you will see clearly to remove the speck from your brother's eye.

Even if today I have intentionally placed myself on a path that makes me more than just a racial justice bystander, care must be taken in any consideration to have others join me on this journey. It is tempting to judge others who perhaps are not keeping pace or not on a similar path. Another perplexing issue is that there was hardly any racial justice support or teaching coming from Catholic Church pulpits, and that situation continues to this day despite the 2018 Bishops' letters on racism and preceding others like it.

The period from 1990-1995 was extremely full in many other ways during our time downstate and then I experienced the second major nineties ODR experience: retiring from RTC in 1995 after twenty-seven years before moving back to Rochester with my family. Yet another separation and renewal sequence began by re-building and restoring bridges with our former lives in Rochester while staying connected with some friends in Goshen.

Unfortunately, this began with the most severe type of separation i.e., the passing of three close friends including Fr. Tony, which was a very tough loss for me and the family. He died of an aggressive neurological disease a few months before we moved back. We returned for his funeral and, at the church, just before they closed the casket, a nun approached us and told us that she had a letter that our son Andrew had recently written his godfather Tony. I took Andrew up to the casket and he placed the letter next to Tony just before it was closed. That was a poignant moment for all of us.

After leaving RTC, I began a telecommunications consulting firm which subsequently merged with another group of ex-RTC veterans before joining forces with some other former RTC colleagues in a tech start-up company. Even though I was in transition (i.e., liminal space) from a career standpoint and thought that my professional career was destined to continue in the new and exploding world of telecom, that was not to be the case. As part of my consulting work and volunteer pursuits, I reconnected with several community-based organizations, including the United Way, and was also elected to the council of our new parish but for a variety of reasons decided not to accept it.

The nineties closed somewhat back at ground zero geographically but with an expanded career opportunity based on my overall experience portfolio. I was also about to discover in the upcoming two decades how my social justice path, even though primarily focused on charitable works twenty years earlier, was about to reconnect in incredible ways and provide a whole new way of looking at the world. These were bridges that I had built over the years that I was now about to cross over.

Two other activities I got involved with consumed a good portion of my community life in the last part of the decade and carried over into the next. The first was the Stephen Ministry program offered by the parish we were attending at the time. I went through an intensive training program after which Stephen Ministers provided high-quality, one-on-one, Christ-centered care to people in the congregation and the community who were experiencing life difficulties.

It was a personal renewal of sorts at the grassroots level: engaging people within the challenges they were experiencing and filling their need for someone to listen with compassion and empathy. Upon reflection, I was honored to have become a Stephen Minister, as it exemplified for me the striking blessings within the old adage of giving and receiving, both for those in need of a sympathetic ear as well as for my fellow Stephen Ministers.

The second activity brought about a reconnection with my grade school music teacher and choir director, Sr. Claudia. She was now using her birth name of Sr. Virginia Hogan and was the musical director and conductor for the Genesee Valley Orchestra and Chorus (GVOC), which she had founded. I had called GVOC's main number simply looking for general information and I didn't know it at the time, but it was Virginia who had answered the phone. Before I knew it, I was at a practice, then singing at concerts, and eventually nominated as president (once again) of her choir. It is amazing how serendipitous the universe is — and how persistent she was!

There was another Oliver North-type family experience during the 1992 Clinton election season. I won't bother with the details, but I later discovered that I had participated in feeding a void in the spirit of harmony. It was not until the last couple of years that I discovered my own sin of silence and how this passivity made me complicit in fostering racism and other injustices. It took me a long time to find my true voice and now my indifference and obliviousness have been unshackled.

Two key questions remain: why this took so long and why others remain constricted. One possible answer that I can attest to personally is fear: fear of change, confrontation, rejection, shame, admitting guilt, denial, and more. How I overcame these fears will be explored more in depth later, but two of the keys were building new relationships, or reconnecting with older ones, and being open to truly listen to their stories. Only by opening our ears to the "others" and listening to their experiences will the "Eureka!" moments occur. Only then will we begin to understand privilege and its roots in white supremacy.

With that thought in mind, what words of advice would I give to my almost fifty-three-year-old self at the conclusion of the decade? My response would be to be mindful of engaging, listening, and actively participating with people who are different than yourself. You will be the one enriched and perhaps better able to understand the plights of so many in this country, based on recent headlines:

- "Black Lieutenant Pepper-Sprayed by Police" (4/13/21, *US News*)
- "Asian American Christians confront racism and evangelical 'purity culture' after Atlanta spa shootings" (4/6/21, *LA Times*)
- "Doormen fired for failing to intervene in anti-Asian attack" (4/7/21, *NY Times*)

Incidents such as these happen multiple times every day in the US. In the nineties, there was not the social media deluge we get today, but such injustices were occurring at the same rate. The "through line" of this memoir, my social and racial justice journey, was still in its infancy, as the testimony of this chapter underscores. Therefore, another piece of advice I would provide is to get at the root causes of incidents involving people like Rodney King and Walter McMillian and explore more in depth how the criminal justice system has failed them — and all of us — so miserably. If I had done this, I would have been much farther along on my journey.

A connection of the King and Simpson events to the Frederick Douglass quote at the beginning of this chapter is highlighted in the following link: https://www.theatlantic.com/culture/archive/2020/06/riots-are-american-way-george-floyd-protests/612466. Fast forward to 2020-2021 with the George Floyd murder and the Capitol insurrection and do your own reflections and comparisons.

Chapter 6
The 2000s: The Way

AUTHOR SUBMISSION

The author on the Camino de Santiago, Spain, in October 2001.

"We are not human beings having a spiritual experience. We are spiritual beings having a human experience." (Pierre Teilhard de Chardin)

"We are not headed toward a single goal: we are on a pilgrimage toward the center of our hearts. It is in this place of prayerful repose that joy unspeakable erupts." (Barbara Holmes)

"There has generally been no conception at all that the white man had anything to learn from [Blacks]. And now, the irony is that [Blacks are] offering the white man a 'message of salvation,' but the white man is so blinded by his self-sufficiency and self-conceit that he does not recognize the peril in which he puts himself by ignoring the offer." (Thomas Merton, Seeds of Destruction)

PEOPLE AND EVENTS IN THE NEWS, 2000-2009: "Y2K," "9/11," WTC, Bin Laden, Afghanistan, Iraq War, weapons of mass destruction, Saddam Hussein, Al-Qaeda, War on Terror, Patriot Act, anthrax, Mumbai, Mexican Drug War, other wars, "Hanging Chad," Bush/Cheney, Obama/Biden, Oscar Grant III, Tea Party, Katrina, Indonesia tsunami, SARS, swine flu, Dot-com bubble burst, housing/credit crisis, foreclosures, bailouts, Great Recession, genome sequencing, Al Gore, global warming, climate change, Mars, mobile phones, texting, smartphones, Google, Facebook, Twitter, GPS, flat screens, Blu-Ray, Native American Apology Resolution

The period of 2000-2009 transitioned us into the twenty-first century, beginning with "Y2K." Our lives were changed forever with the many tumultuous events that followed after surviving the scare of a somewhat anticipated technology meltdown. For me, there would be significant intersectionality with the forthcoming, incredible national disasters, both spiritually and financially, as well as experiencing a serious health event. So, order, disorder, reorder (ODR) patterns continued to flow, change, and interfere with what were thought to be the norms as we began a new millennium. Simply reread the list above if you need any more proof. You could also fast forward twenty years to our ongoing time of COVID-19 for additional validation.

This would be the decade that, after thirty-five years in the telecommunications industry, I switched gears and transitioned into the world of non-profits. Moving into this sector was relatively seamless for a variety of reasons, not the least of which were my experiences and the numerous contacts I had made over the years. Little did I know that this career change would lead to many more enriching experiences and new, "out of my comfort zone" relationships over the next two decades.

My first "toe in the water" so to speak happened under somewhat serendipitous circumstances. Our youngest son had recently entered McQuaid Jesuit, my high school alma mater, and a new president had just been installed who just happened to be a former colleague and friend of mine at RTC. We ran into each other early in my son's freshman year and he indicated that his former job at McQuaid as head of advancement was still open. One thing led to another, and a few months later I was selected to fill that position. This circumstance of converging events was a harbinger of how subsequent job changes occurred with two other non-profits over the course of the next ten years that changed the course of my life.

I will eventually get into the significance of this career shift, but there was another experience that was perhaps one of the most important in my life. While I was wrapping up the final stages of my telecom career in early 2001, and again by happenstance versus intent, I learned about an ancient, over 1,000-year-old pilgrimage in northern Spain: the now well-known Camino de Santiago.

The cover story of an AARP magazine edition in late 2000/early 2001 featured actress Shirley MacLaine and her book, *The Way*, about her recent pilgrimage walking the Camino. She experienced an intense spiritual and physical challenge on a grueling trip on foot that lasted a month. For some reason, I was intrigued by this article, and I eventually read her book. In writing this memoir, I dug deeper into what may have drawn me to learn more about the Camino.

I was in my early fifties, married over twenty-five years, with two kids graduated from college and another soon to be in high school, had a thirty-year professional career, was financially secure, yet there seemed to be a "nudging" to do something beyond my comfort zone. I may have pondered some questions such as "Now, beyond the midpoint of my life, what do I really know about life, my inner self, my faith, God?" and "Have I merely drifted along within life's circumstances?"

There was undoubtedly something stirring inside me along the lines of these questions, but I did not know exactly what, nor what to do about it. I pushed the Camino back into the recesses of my mind, like many other things, as something to consider when I retired or perhaps on a vacation with Sandy sometime. It wasn't until a few months later in 2001 when an opportunity arose to consider the possibility of taking what I called a sabbatical.

I was moving on from a telecom position with a start-up company and began to explore a possible move into the non-profit sector. A window of several weeks opened and a thought occurred that it might be possible to carve out some time during the late summer/early fall to do something unique. I was thinking this would ideally include meeting different people, facing a physical challenge, and experiencing spiritual renewal. This is precisely what the Camino offered, including the extra bonus of ample religious history — and not just Catholic. However, the Camino did not re-enter my mind until early that summer when I overheard a woman in a health club talking about it.

A two-month roller coaster sequence of events began. I did some initial research about the Camino and determined that late September through October would be the best time to go for a variety of reasons. Then, Sandy fell and broke her wrist, requiring surgery and rehab. If I was to do anything, she would not be able to join me. However, both Sandy and our children were modestly relentless that, if I wanted to do this, I should go.

I demurred and went ahead and made travel arrangements but was still looking for some sign or reason not to go. Nothing came up, so I bought my hiking gear but put it aside, looking for a reason to take it back. Nothing happened, and even though I was in relatively good shape, I had to see if I was capable of walking twenty miles a day, so I began some training. This took me to early September and I still thought it was no better than a 50/50 chance I would go. My mind was on Sandy's broken wrist, but I admit there was also some fear of the unknown, being on my own in a foreign country and essentially being out of my comfort zone.

Ten days before I was supposed to depart, the tragic events of 9/11 happened. This was horrific on so many levels, primarily the lives lost and the countless others devastated. But I persevered, primarily due to Sandy's and my family's support and my heightened resoluteness that I was not going to be deterred as long as the planes were able to fly. I departed on schedule, which was fortunate given the international security circumstances prevailing at the time. The five-week experience was more than a long vacation or getaway, and it could be a book in and of itself since the journal I kept is over 100 pages. The following is a summary of what I experienced:

• A profound connection to "9/11" prevailed throughout those five weeks, intensified by the fact that my youngest son and I were in New York City three days before the tragedy struck. We were there for a long weekend, attended a Yankees game, and stayed at the Marriott World Trade Center Hotel, which was destroyed as part of the towers collapsed just three days later. So, like many others, 9/11 was very personal. I was one of few Americans at the time who even knew about the Camino (this year marks the 20th anniversary of my walk) so I met only a handful of fellow citizens. However, when other pilgrims found out I was American, the typical response was one of deep remorse and authentic consolation.

• There was a pre-Camino miracle of sorts the day before I left to walk "The Way." My daughter was hired for her first professional position, and I was offered a job with a telecom consulting firm, to begin upon my return. My entry into the non-profit sector would have to wait for another two years. This began an interesting sequence of circumstances over the next three days, before I began my walk, including one in Pamplona, Spain. I was looking for travel information and was having difficulty finding the symbol *"I"* in a plaza fortuitously named after St. Francis of Assisi, who was also a pilgrim (*peregrino*) on the Camino hundreds of years earlier. I changed my perspective by standing in front of his statue and eventually followed the direction his hand was pointing and toward where his renowned wolf companion, Gubbio, was looking. Lo and behold, there was the "I." Lesson learned: a change of perspective can make a difference and, secondly, be alert to the markers on your path. This was an important reminder for me as I embarked on a 500-mile walk, as well as for life in general.

• This "path" can be at any given time a paved road, one with stone, gravel, sand, dirt (or mud if raining), farmland or a cow path, a creek, traverse over three or four mountain ranges (including the Pyrenees) and some desert type terrain as well. Challenges abound, but people of all ages walk it — some with limiting physical challenges.

• When I walked the Camino twenty years ago, the pilgrims were primarily middle-aged, white females and males from across the world. I recall hardly any Black pilgrims. This could have been driven by the time of year, since the summer draws far more people than the fall. There are also many bikers who do the Camino, as well as some on horseback.

• The Camino is "the way" or the path leading to the purported burial site of St. James (or *Santiago*, therefore the name of the city). He was one of Jesus' twelve apostles and whom Jesus called upon to do "Acts of the Apostles" work in the Iberian Peninsula (modern Spain and Portugal). He was martyred in Jerusalem, and his remains, as legend has it, found their way back to the northwest coast of Spain. They have been interred for roughly 1,000 years in the Cathedral of Santiago de Compostela. Ever since, millions of pilgrims from across the world have walked to what is considered one of Christianity's holiest sites. A fitting definition of "pilgrim" is a "traveler praying with his or her feet" and, based on that interpretation, I said a few million prayers over my four-week, 500-mile trek!

• The communal aspects of the Camino went beyond walking and included routine opportunities to have discussions over meals. Overnight accommodations were called albergues or refugios, where I typically heard snoring in many different languages. Over time, I became good friends with several people from France and one Basque Spaniard. We overcame language barriers and we each had our moments to help out in various situations. I knew some Spanish and French, and my English was useful at times, so I was able to hold my own.

• Although there were significant religious aspects to this challenging walk, it was distinctly a spiritual experience for me. I had many conversations with God along "the way" and I realized that, for me, walking is the preferred mode of prayer. My comfort zone for prayer leans heavily to the internal. Even today, my typical three-to-four-mile daily walks allow the freedom and time to express myself.

• There were several more physical manifestations of the spiritual, such as the markers (i.e., usually yellow painted arrows primarily on buildings or on the roads) that kept pilgrims on the right path. They became like blessings and, when I saw them, I would usually do the sign of the cross with my walking stick in thanksgiving. Also, "angels" popped up routinely: other pilgrims, villagers, and unseen others who provided assistance in extraordinary and unexpected ways; the thousands of "footprints" imprinted on my heart and soul and not just simply experienced on the path; my shadow that kept me company whenever I saw it.

• I began to wonder whether the numerous coincidences and "miracles" that occurred before I even left the States were simply circumstantial or meant to keep me on my toes. Being alert for special markers or people is something that has carried forward to this day, and I try not to take them for granted. Everything, good or bad, has a purpose, with some having a deeper meaning than others. I

110

truly believe that everything and everyone are markers on our life's journey, in some form or another.

• It should be noted that the religious and historical significance of the Camino encompasses not just Catholics but the Jewish and Islamic faiths. Spain represents a crossroads for all three of these important world religions, going back over two millennia.

• There was ample time for contemplation as we were spread out on the path, as well as limited by language barriers. To be "in the moment," I purposely did not wear a watch and haven't since. Despite this, it remains a challenge for me not to dwell on either past failures or future hopes, and to be fully present with whatever and whomever. To the extent I can think or even write about it suggests that I am conscious of being present, especially regarding patient listening, which I find myself continuously working on. To this day, I occasionally call on my Camino adventure to help me become a better listener. Authentic listening is one of the best examples of presence. A great example of this in practice has been the many dialogues I have been blessed to experience with my many Black brothers and sisters. The Camino paid itself forward on my current racial and justice journey.

In concluding this section on one of the most indelible and spiritual experiences of my life, a couple of reflective questions come to mind: Why did I even think of attempting this journey of hundreds of miles, thousands of miles away from home and on my own in the first place, and how was I changed? One way to answer the first question is through using the metaphor of the mountain ranges I traversed on the Camino, with all the associated climbing and descending required, and compare those challenges to the several ODR up and down cycles in my life.

What I saw at the age of fifty-four was an opportunity to take a step back from my routine vantage point (or comfort zone) developed over my life through the ODR sequences described in the previous chapters. I had arrived at a point of trying to dig deeper into who my true self was, where I might be heading, and to also consider exposing and testing my humanity and vulnerability more than I ever had before.

As I was writing this, I immediately recollected the famous prayer of Thomas Merton:

My Lord God, I have no idea where I am going. I do not see the road ahead of me. I cannot know for certain where it will end. Nor do I think I really know myself, and the fact that I think I am following your will does not mean that I am actually doing so. But I believe that the desire to please you does in fact please you. And I hope I have that desire in all that I am doing. I hope that I will never do anything apart from that desire. And I know that if I do this you will lead me by the right road, though I may know nothing about it. Therefore, I will trust you always though I may seem to be lost and in the shadow of death. I will not fear, for you are ever with me, and you will never leave me to face my perils alone.

I feel this prayer beautifully captures my response to the first question of why. How I was changed has been a frequently asked question even to this day. The Camino provided great reinforcement to the Pierre Teilhard de Chardin concept that I was not a human being having a spiritual experience but a spiritual being having a human experience. I began to better understand my role in the physical world and that the world (God or love) is in me. I am thankful to have Merton's prayer nearby on my bulletin board as an occasional reminder.

At the technical conclusion of the walk, at the cathedral in Santiago, I learned the true meaning of the phrase "Life is a journey and not a destination" when the priest at the closing Mass said that this was not the end of the journey but the beginning of the pilgrimage to the discovery of our authentic heart. Upon my return, within just a few short months, I found out how true his words were.

I had just begun what was to be the last step in my telecom career when the dot.com bubble burst and my investment portfolio took a negative hit, leading us to move once again to downsize and refinance. Straddling all this were some serious health challenges that Sandy faced and my being diagnosed with prostate cancer. This began an even longer journey of months of tests and radiation treatments I fittingly labeled my "Camino II."

Sandy wanted to immediately share my diagnosis with our extended family and friends to ask for their prayers. Although appreciative of the power associated with prayer, I was reticent until I had the chance to determine the exact treatment protocol I was going to use. Until that was identified, I did not want to be distracted by having to respond to the obvious questions that would be forthcoming. That being said, and given the significance of a cancer diagnosis, prayer was essential and would ultimately bear fruit as Camino II progressed.

This period could be yet another book on its own due to the many ups and downs, new "angels," and other circumstances. Based on my extensive research, I decided to go to a center of radiation excellence in Georgia after a strong recommendation from a college roommate who was a physician. Even though the logistics were going to be extremely challenging, I had matters worked out relatively quickly. Then, I called our attorney, a high school classmate, about our plans to move and mentioned some relative urgency due to my upcoming radiation treatments out of town. He immediately started saying a prayer over the phone and invited me to a weekly men's group meeting at his house for a healing service, saying they would be fasting for me before we came together.

I was blown away, fasted myself, and went two times to his house for healing services. After this sequence, I asked myself what I was going to do now? Had I been healed? What about my plans to go to Georgia for two months? How do I even begin to explain this to anyone without them thinking me crazy?

I contacted my primary care provider, asked his advice (he did not think I was crazy), and he suggested that I go see a renowned local urologist. He listened patiently, was very open to updated testing, and even though he leaned heavily toward surgery he completely understood my rationale for going with radiation therapy. Sandy and I gave it forty-eight hours of prayerful discernment and decided to abandon the Georgia plan and stay in Rochester for the next testing and treatment steps with him. To summarize all this, I had one friend who helped me out immensely in my initial research, then another who provided a healing intervention which, even though did not heal me, it contributed to me not being apart from my family for a considerable time. This was another sequence of "angels" entering my Camino II path. There were several others. The result was a positive medical outcome that has thankfully been sustained now for almost twenty years.

Taken together, both Camino experiences occurred within twelve to fourteen months and provided yet another highly charged ODR and liminal sequence in my life. Within that time, I walked the Camino, started a new job, suffered some financial setbacks, Sandy experienced some major health events, I received a cancer diagnosis and associated treatment, and we sold and bought two houses. Order, disorder, reorder, and transition were in high gear!

As I was beginning to write this paragraph I again got stuck and asked myself, "So what is the true connection of this ODR sequence that fits with what I am trying to communicate overall?" I let it rest for a day or so and then a thought mysteriously came to mind that my Camino journal might hold the key. I turned to the back pages where I discovered some thoughts that I forgot I had written regarding my "second Camino." Contained in my writings, right under my nose, were some connecting points that clarified what I should write about:

• I had some notes mentioning "the edge," which I believe was a reference to some books and music I was listening to at the time of my cancer treatments. I wrote this: "'Come to the edge', he said. They said: 'We are afraid'. 'Come to the edge', he said. They came. He pushed them … and they flew." (Christopher Logue)

• Coincidentally, on the first page of the journal were some inspirational quotes from the author David Whyte I had jotted down to provide encouragement during my Camino walk. "Perhaps the pilgrimage is right here; wherever our edge of understanding has been established is the very place we should look more intently, but it is also the place that fills us most with fear; I do not have to overcome fears but simply know what I am afraid of."

• The "edge" and "cliff" analogies are appropriate in the context of the jump I took into the non-profit sector after thirty-five years in telecom, which then led to the even bigger leap into social and racial justice advocacy after I retired in 2014.

In presenting this now, I am somewhat overwhelmed at the unbelievable similarity of thought, how prescient these words were, and how I continue to be blessed today with the wisdom they provide. It was not until over ten years later that I discovered the mortar to fill the cracks of my growing spirituality i.e., Fr. Richard Rohr.

However, I know that, whether poetry or my own Camino journal notes, comfort and support were provided during a time of many uncertainties in my life, including facing a cancer diagnosis that went beyond surviving and turned me into a cancer "thriver!"Some readers of the health journey I have just described, including its successful outcome, might ask, "What about me?" in connection with access to the medical expertise I was blessed to have. Like the many manifestations of unequal care during the current COVID pandemic, this inequality is a matter of grave concern no matter what the color of your skin. Thankfully, the national 2010 Affordable Care Act has begun to improve inequities, especially with the BIPOC communities, but there is a long way to go.

Overlapping this period was a fair amount of discernment regarding a career change that happened in 2004. Accepting the position at McQuaid began a ten-year second career in the non-profit world and, due to the initial learning curve and the work demands, basically "took the oxygen out of the room" with respect to other outside board, community, and parish activities. Reconnecting with my Jesuit roots at McQuaid for over four years was a great experience, not only because our son was attending there, but also because I was able to refresh and learn even more about Jesuit theology and philosophy. Additionally, McQuaid became a surrogate for parish-type ministry, which was interestingly the reverse of my high school experience.

After I left McQuaid in 2008, I accepted the executive director position at Cornell Cooperative Extension of Monroe County (CCEMC), where I worked until 2012, when I accepted a position at Catholic Family Center. This immersion into non-profits also opened the door to many new relationships and reconnecting with a few important others; the combination of each of these served as a dynamic springboard to what happened after I retired in 2014 (although I never used the "r" word officially for several years). It also should be noted that my non-profit work during this period was mostly related to fundraising and other more secular pursuits rather than anything directly related to social and racial justice. However, it provided a foundation for that work, just a few years away, and contributed to my ever-evolving network.

My entry into the non-profit world was consistent with one important element of the business sector I left after thirty-five years:

its dominant, institutional whiteness and white culture, all boiled in the pot of something most whites do not want to admit: white supremacy. The leadership, staffing, and students at McQuaid were overwhelmingly white. This was even further demonstrated at CCE-MC, which brought me into a statewide system of virtually complete whiteness at the executive director level of over fifty county directors and county officials, although it should be noted that its overall leader was a Black female.

The depth of this cannot be overstated, since most local non-profit organizations were led by white males and females controlling millions of revenue dollars. This is not to say that the work, services, and programs provided were being stewarded poorly, but more suggesting that important other voices and opinions were hardly ever heard at the decision table, including how dollars were spent and hiring practices.

A lifelong legacy was sustaining itself during this decade: born into whiteness, educated and churched into the depths of white history while ignorant of other narratives, hired into a white-dominated business culture, and then this same culture sustained in the non-profit sector. Whether it be access to white collar jobs, the doors that opened automatically without question for volunteer board positions, or opportunities presented for wealth creation, the unearned privileges I was born with multiplied over the course of my life simply because I was white.

This perspective evaded me during my career change into the non-profit sector and my white obliviousness endured until years later. Did that make me or any other white person reading this with a similar life story a bad person? Looking back, I feel I was robbed of having a more robust, diverse, and participative life experience if the true history had been presented and discussed more broadly and accurately.

But this is providing a self-serving excuse and does not go far enough as it suggests a passive role of a more accurate history not being made visible to me. Is that my privilege showing? Could I claim I was blinded by the startling glare of whiteness over most of my life? In hindsight, I was perhaps as responsible as my parents, teachers, bosses, and society at large for not being more engaged and aware of what was happening around me.

Why didn't my ears really hear what Dr. King was saying during the Civil Rights movement? Why didn't my eyes notice the people who were being attacked by police dogs over the decades; why didn't I encourage participation of more people of color into the church, community, or business discussions I was involved with over the years?

At this point, I want to express an opinion as well as a confession that will probably make many white readers flinch: my passivity, self-absorption, and complicit silence regarding white supremacy over most of my life has contributed to the tremendous social and political divide we have today in 2021. A very small part of my self-imposed penance for these sins of omission is in the form of quotes I used at the end of all my e-mails for a couple of years:

• "Unity is created out of diversity" (1 Corinthians 12:12-27); Latin translation: "e pluribus unum"

• "Few are guilty, but all are responsible." (Rabbi Abraham Joshua Heschel)

• "It's easier to build strong children than to repair broken men." (Frederick Douglass)

• "America stands for freedom, liberty and justice for all. And it's not happening for all right now." (Colin Kaepernick)

• "When you are accustomed to privilege, equality feels like oppression." (Oscar Auliq-ice)

I selected these out of many possibilities to communicate wisdom and hope and perhaps lead to deeper understanding. The responses I occasionally received were overwhelmingly positive, but there were some surprising exceptions.

This segues into how white supremacy has intersected with my social and racial justice journey. An oft used ad hominem expression one of my relatives poses occasionally is "How dare you?" when doing something such as promoting, assisting, or participating in today's Black Lives Matter (BLM) movement. My response to this, in the spirit of not being complicit by silence, is "How do I dare not take up the cause of the downtrodden in accordance with the Eight Beatitudes?

As this narrative has exposed, a lifetime passed by before I finally began to overtake my passivity and hesitation through more active participation and advocacy in what I would call the patriotic pursuit of social and racial justice. For example, I am currently "taking back" the American flag by holding a small one together with a BLM sign at weekly BLM rallies coordinated by a local group, Elders and Allies, together with the Sisters of St. Joseph (SSJ) and Mercy ... in the spirit of "liberty and justice for all." Elders and Allies formed after the local killing of Daniel Prude by police and is comprised of respected community leaders, not necessarily senior citizens.

We simply stand peacefully at busy street intersections in silence for an hour, holding our signs and flags as a model of non-violent advocacy. The next chapter will more fully reveal similar action steps anyone can do to make a difference simply by being present, just as SSJs from Rochester did in 1965 in Selma, Alabama, when they tended to the seriously injured future Congressman John Lewis at the "Bloody Sunday" protest.

Another thought about BLM: some of the controversy surrounding the name, beyond the fact that its importance is in it being as much or more of a movement as opposed to an organization, is that there's an important word absent yet implied: too. Simply stated, Black Lives Matter too! — not other lives do not matter. When I sometimes hear All Lives Matter! or Blue Lives Matter! shouted back at rallies, those words go without saying and, frankly, those types of shoutouts are dismissive of racism. The implied message of "too" is essential with BLM due to this country's 400-year history of demonstrating just the opposite i.e., that Black lives do *not* matter.

This is not an attempt to justify the damage done by the riots of 2020, but they represent the language of the unheard that white America has for the most part failed to hear. After the Capitol insurrection on January 6, 2021, if this country could not see it before, we now have a vivid portrayal of the divided America we live in. How we begin to cross that abyss is a question for all Americans to consider.

To briefly touch upon some more personal aspects of what occurred in the 2000s, my mother passed away in 2006 at the age of eighty-eight, our two oldest children got married, our first grandchild was born, and our youngest began college. Obviously, these and other events were life-changing touchstones and I simply mention them for the important context they provided to my life at the time.

My mother's passing was particularly poignant and like when my father passed forty years earlier; I was with the same brother but this time in a different hospital in the Adirondacks. The following day, after my other siblings arrived, I coordinated a prayer service at her favorite Catholic church that began a sequence of two wakes and her funeral in Rochester. We keep a small lamp lit in my mother's memory so that her "light" remains shining.

In the opening of this chapter, the last item mentioned is the "Native American Apology Resolution" (see appendix) signed by President Obama in 2009. I bring this up for a variety of reasons, primarily based on my St. Bonaventure University background. The nickname used by the school's sports teams at the time I attended was the "Brown Indian" and was represented by two student mascots in "chief" and "squaw" costumes. In the early nineties, the Brown Indian became a symbol of concern for the university as a new era of cultural sensitivity arose across the nation over the inappropriate use of Native American names and imagery.

This new awareness shed light on how the offensive appropriation of Native culture was harmful to Native Americans attempting to reclaim their identity and respect by halting the perpetuation of outdated stereotypes. Many professional sports teams and universities began to alter their names and team mascots and these changes continue today. The Bonaventure mascot is now a wolf, a reference to the Wolf of Gubbio, a story from the life of St. Francis and mentioned earlier in this chapter.

There remains, however, much more to tell. At the time, I resisted this shift and went so far as to purchase a T-shirt stating something like "Brown Indians Forever!" Worse, it did not even register with me until years later how inappropriate it was that a "hanging tree" was used during the undefeated basketball season my senior year in 1968 to "lynch" a replica of the opposing team's mascot. Hundreds of students cheered this celebration after every home victory. Obviously, I still had a long way to even come close to an appreciation as to what social and racial justice really entailed and overcome my white supremacist roots.

So, to my Indigenous brothers and sisters, I owe you my personal apology, in addition to the national one issued in 2009. In that spirit, I offer two Wabanaki terms: N'dilnabamuk ("all my relations"), used at the end of prayers in honor of the importance of all creations' relationships; and Kciye ("harmony with the natural world"), meaning the obligation to care for all creation in the same way that we would care for our human relatives. Hopefully this modest tribute offers some small recompense to my dishonor.

As 2010 approached, there were three major national events that happened: the 2007- 2008 financial crisis, which subsequently led to the Great Recession and was a contributing factor in the election of President Barack Obama in 2008. The bursting of the housing bubble, subprime and predatory lending practices, lax credit scrutiny, and many other factors led to the financial crisis. The Great Recession followed and officially lasted from December 2007 to June 2009, yet it took many more years for the economy to recover due in part to households and financial institutions paying off debts accumulated in the years preceding the crisis. The combination of this financial havoc with other political issues of the day provided a perfect storm for the McCain Republican presidential campaign and Obama was elected in a decisive victory.

I would like to capsulize my thoughts on these three important events:

• Based on historical facts, I do not think there is any argument that the poor and POC suffered disproportionate egregious financial pain and insecurity associated with the financial crisis and Great Recession. Fast forward to the current pandemic and the heightened racial injustice dilemma relative to infections and deaths, and you can observe the consistent thread of racism that has existed since this country's creation. The white dominated system (white supremacy) I believe is fundamentally responsible for this continuing disproportionality, which is a crisis in itself.

• Many whites believed that, by Obama being elected, the country had somehow miraculously moved to what was labeled then as our new, "post-racial" era. History suggests that this was a huge overreach of reality that the first Black president could by himself move the country forward into such an era, given the white supremist foundational roots of the country going back over 400 years and the associated institutional racism which continues to expand insidiously.

• The Obama years began to open my eyes to not only what was possible but what was necessary regarding racial justice; but again, I

120

must admit that I was still stuck in my instinctively white patterns of perspective and behavior and only skimmed the surface, blissfully unaware of the depths of the problem.

• I now realize that my white and other privileges allowed me immunity. I almost had to file for unemployment after leaving Mc-Quaid, but doors were opened providing me the opportunity to seamlessly start a new position at CCEMC. Fortunately we did not have a mortgage, and even though my 401(k) took a big hit, it did not have the impact compared to the tech implosion years earlier. In relatively short order, the portfolio was restored to its previous level and began growing again. It should be noted that disproportionality prevails when you compare white access to such wealth creation opportunities to that of POC. One should not have to dig too deep to determine the root causes of this: inherent and systemic access inequities versus privileges whites enjoy regarding education, housing, jobs, health care, and more.

I did not recognize it at the time, but these events served as a harbinger of what was to come over the next ten years. They served as a backdrop and were somewhat foundational to my social and racial justice journey, which was about to get considerably more active. And so, what words of advice would I give to my almost sixty-three-year-old self at the conclusion of the decade?

I am currently reading President Obama's memoir, *A Promised Land,* and the extreme partisanship he encountered early on and throughout his presidency is striking in its unfortunate similarity to the politics of today. Even some of the key people involved are the same. The advice I would offer to myself is to suggest following Obama's example of not losing heart or becoming discouraged and to trek on like when I faced challenges on the Camino.

The focus should be on the end game (the Cathedral), with a tangential reminder to stay in the moment and remain steady on an honorable path. This becomes challenging when one inevitably comes up against complex obstacles, situations, or people. It is very easy to be disheartened and lose hope.

Forgiveness also comes to mind, especially starting with yourself when you stumble or fail to live up to your own standards. This will substantially assist in modeling conversations with others who may have unwittingly, or perhaps knowingly, impeded your path. Since I continue to struggle with this, I can honestly say I wish I had someone tell me this over ten years ago. To forgive in a "70 x 7" context is easy to say and another thing to do. So, my last tip is as exclaimed on the Camino, Ultreya! or "Go forward with courage!"

Part II

Chapter 7
2010-2019: Connecting, Reconnecting, Interconnectedness

PIXABAY

Connecting the dots.

"You have to trust that the dots will somehow connect in your future. You have to trust in something — your gut, destiny, life, karma, whatever. Because believing that the dots will connect down the road will give you the confidence to follow your heart..."
(Steve Jobs)

"Those who say, 'I love God,' and hate their brothers or sisters, are liars; for those who do not love a brother or sister whom they have seen, cannot love God whom they have not seen." (1 John 4:20)

PEOPLE AND EVENTS IN THE NEWS, 2010-2019: Trayvon Martin, Eric Garner, Michael Brown, George Floyd, Philando Castile, Alton Sterling, Freddie Gray, Tamir Rice, and the 4,000+ who preceded them via lynching and ongoing police related killings, BLM, white supremacy, Occupy Wall Street, Affordable Care Act, Pope Francis, Brexit, Hillary, "45," Obama/Biden, ISIS, Russian Hack, Ukraine, Impeachment, Philippine Typhoon, global warming, wildfires, Haiti/Japan earthquakes, Paris Climate Agreement, hurricanes, Bin Laden, mass shootings, Ebola, LGBTQ, "Me Too," Arab Spring, Charleston/AME, Charlottesville, Saint Kateri Tekak-witha, child sex abuse scandals, "Green Book," "12 Years a Slave," El Paso, family border separations, "Truth and Facts," United States Conference of Catholic Bishops' Letter on Racism, 1619 Project.

Since the title of this chapter is about "connecting the dots," I want to give a little nod to the power of networks in my life and how they mysteriously and organically created other "connections" and "dots," both in personal relationships as well as with formal and informal organizations. The combination of my Catholic roots and experiences, alumni contacts, diverse career path, community/volunteer work, and personal friendships have all led to a confluence of innumerable relationships and networks. As I observed on the Camino, a few stuck, but others changed and moved on to allow others to enter. I have been blessed, enriched, and energized by them all and I consider them to be miracles and "angels" and not just mere happenstance.

The importance of building new and diverse relationships (dots) cannot be understated in the context of why I decided to write this memoir. You can choose to watch as many race-related programs on TV or at the movies, read books, attend programs, conferences, listen to sermons etc. But until you really know someone and a little about their experiences, none of those other things are as powerful as their stories. In the case of Black relationships, I can honestly say that, prior to 2014, I had many Black or POC work colleagues, employees, and those I knew casually through the community, but I didn't really have what I could call a Black friend or close acquaintance. Today, I have over two dozen, including two Black females who are among my closest friends. I am in contact with them regularly and we know much about each other's stories and experiences.

As one of these friends, Judy Toyer, told us recently, "Thanks to you and Sandy for saying 'Yes' to the call to do this most challenging and difficult work of God. You might consider speaking on your activism for racial and social justice as a 'spiritual practice' in which you have engaged." I am in effect speaking by writing this book. I should also mention that, in the developing days of our friendship when I told Judy I really appreciated that she was willing to share some of her life experience as a Black female from the South, she returned the favor by telling me something I will always remember.

She told me that, since whites were always in control in her early life, she had always thought their acts intentional and deliberate. Until we began a dialogue, Judy was unaware of the depth of white ignorance of the Black experience in this country. Again, this is not an excuse for the behavior, but a starting point in understanding how far we have to go — and how many are waiting for whites to come from behind.

The phrase "connecting the dots" suggests that awareness doesn't happen on its own but must intentionally and with authenticity be activated. Judy advised me that perhaps this is a personal, informal ministry that I have developed over the years. When she told me this, I recalled what I wrote in the seventies chapter about my experience with the Black female supervisor and my dinner invitation.

I have paid that experience forward innumerable times since, through informal, relaxed meetings with people of all races and colors, male and female and it has enriched my life in many ways. In a pre-COVID world, I would typically have one-on-one, early morning breakfast conversations a couple of times a week with old friends, or perhaps meet people for the first time, usually at one of several local Paneras. This is just one way to begin to build relationships and make new connections.

I began writing Part II with this chapter on January 18, 2021, which was coincidentally Martin Luther King Jr. Day, the eve of my seventy-fourth birthday, two days before President Biden's inauguration, and just two weeks after the horror of the Capitol insurrection on January 6.

In Dr. King's 1963 "Letter from a Birmingham Jail," he wrote these timeless words: "We are caught in an inescapable network of mutuality, tied in a single garment of destiny." I thought this quote was in keeping with the title of this chapter, as well as Fr. Richard Rohr's words "we need a delivery system in the world to provide the capacity for building bridges and connecting the dots of life." I cannot think of two better people from whom to draw inspiration for Part II (perhaps more appropriately titled "Act II" of this narrative).

Entering this decade, I did not realize that 1947-2009 was just one long, expansive "Order" sequence suffused with white oblivious-ness that was yet four years away from changing.

After leading CCEMC until early 2012, I was hired by Catholic Family Center (CFC) as development director. CFC had been the parent of CYO and eventually absorbed most of its programs. This brought me full circle from my board work in the eighties, but this time on a paid basis. It happened as a direct result of reconnecting with two friends from my time with the CYO Board and Catholic Charities. My work in the eighties continued to bear fruit almost thirty years later.

The initial four years of the decade resulted in three more grand-children, the college graduation of our youngest, who then went on to post-graduate work as well as a Peace Corps experience in the Philippines. Sandy and I visited him there and were shocked to see some of the poorest living conditions in the world. We saw firsthand the potential impact of climate change on an impoverished nation comprised of thousands of islands, the conditions somewhat offset by a highly resilient, Catholic population. I recalled an eerily similar encounter with another poverty-stricken area, almost forty years to the day earlier. Sandy and I were being driven to our honeymoon resort on the Caribbean island of St. Lucia. On a mountain road at dusk, we observed scantily clad indigenous women and children along the roadside, carrying food, water, and laundry down the trail. The sight tugged on our heartstrings, but not enough to pull us from our tourist/observer status.

During the early part of the decade, we were both involved with managing respective family, elder care situations that demanded a great deal of our time and attention. We considered getting more involved on a volunteer basis with organizations such as Lifespan, but life circumstances moved us in different directions. We both got involved with some fellow parishioners in helping a refugee, sin-gle-parent family of six from Eritrea get settled in the city.

There was an initial six-month period of engagement required through Catholic Family Center protocols when, ostensibly, our work was to be completed. However, after six months the family still had a variety of challenges that could have left them flounder-ing or worse if left completely on their own. Fortunately, Sandy was

126

able to continue to provide ongoing logistical, moral, and empathetic support and nearly five years later she is still connected to what is a flourishing family of potential new citizens. I am very proud of the tremendous work she has done for this family and how they all love her!

In the second chapter I mentioned how, in 2013, I became aware of Fr. Richard Rohr, OFM, an American author, spiritual writer, and Franciscan friar. Since then, I've been receiving his inspiring and transformative daily reflections, have read several of his books, attended some of his online conferences, met him at a live conference in Albuquerque, and saw him speak at the Chautauqua Institute a couple of years ago. Together with a fellow Bonaventure classmate, we began a small men's study group that now meets twice a month to discuss his teachings and philosophy. Our group provides intimate mutual support and, through hour-long discussions, we help each other to stay spiritually grounded.

In late 2014, I was fortunate to return to Spain to walk the last seventy miles of the Camino once more, this time with Sandy, who wanted to have some of the real experience rather than just listening to my stories. We walked on the same path I had traveled over a decade ago. The Camino, with its increased notoriety, was noticeably more crowded with walkers and bikers from all parts of the world. Though we walked "only" eight-to-ten miles a day for a week, the richness of the human exchanges we had were identical to my first time. It was wonderful to be able to share some of my experience with my wife, and every now and then we think about returning.

Another privilege we experienced during the decade was the opportunity to build another house in the suburb of Fairport, on the east side of Rochester. Afterward, I had occasional thoughts of a move back to the city, but our daughter's family was planning on moving nearby and we decided to remain in Fairport. In retrospect, this worked out well with my racial and social justice activities as there were just as many (or more) suburban whites. Sandy and I are essentially growing where we are planted and trying to sow seeds of change and engagement on various justice initiatives.

On the national front, the first four years of the decade saw the end of Obama's first term and the beginning of the second, with the Affordable Care Act (ACA) being one of his crowning achievements despite the political debates that ensued and continue to this day. The primary benefits, from my view, were that the ACA significantly increased Americans' ability to get health care and narrowed racial and ethnic disparities in insurance coverage. Those benefits still enjoy substantial public support and will likely be sustained with the Biden administration.

After I left CFC in mid-2014, I didn't immediately retire and began to engage on a volunteer basis with a new local organization that again connected with Catholic Charities in terms of its initial funding. The Rochester Alliance of Communities Transforming Society, or Roc/ACTS (R/A), is comprised of approximately thirty local faith communities, including various religious denominations. I gradually began to pull away from boards and committees (governance), gravitating to more hands-on work associated with social and racial justice.

That same year, Sandy and I attended the R/A formation ceremony and I became an R/A delegate from our parish in the fall. I soon got involved with several advocacy initiatives, but my interest was focused on a new program R/A was launching called "Sacred Conversations on Race and Action" (SC). The impact of this program would change both Sandy's and my life forever.

SC was developed in Ferguson, Missouri, in 2014 by an interfaith group after the tragic police shooting and death of a young Black male, Michael Brown. In that Rochester is no different than other communities across the country regarding our racial past and ongoing institutional racism, R/A decided in 2015 to implement the program here. SC's mission is for people to learn more about their neighbors ("others"), to encourage them to dig deeper within themselves and confront their own racist apprehensions, to inspire them to action for change and, most importantly, to encourage listening to the stories of Black brothers and sisters.

In the late spring of 2016, our parish, the Church of the Assumption (COTA), became the first white faith community in our diocese to participate in an SC program, together with another Black faith community in the city. It was presented by trained R/A facilitators. I assisted in getting the program off the ground, along with Sandy and thirteen other white participants. The Black, city faith community we partnered with also had fifteen members who attended the two,

128

three-hour sessions at their church led by Rev. Wanda Wilson, who co-facilitated the program.

Sandy and I developed several new relationships and learned a great deal from the traumatic stories shared by the Black participants. Here are some highlights:

- From one of the more creative yet simple exercises, we and the other whites attending were enlightened as to the depth of white privilege and participated in an open discussion with the group.
- We heard the stories of how Black parents and grandparents have "the talk" with their children about what to do if confronted by the police
- We learned how one middle-aged woman, to save her life, was put on a train from her home in the Jim Crow South at a very young age to live with family in Rochester after disrespecting a white clerk by not addressing her properly
- We listened to a story of how one Black woman and her white husband were pulled over by the police — under suspicion that she was a prostitute

There were many other similar stories and we found it impossible to end our connection with this community after the two sessions. We would occasionally go to their Sunday services and attend other social events. This became a routine and, pre-COVID, we attended other Black community Sunday services as well. We were always greeted warmly, with open arms, and thoroughly enjoyed the energy, spirit, and passion of the services and sermons, although not always their length! As whites, we were learning about the deep waters of the American Black Christian faith experience, its energetic music, and remarkable preaching.

Coincident with this 2014-16 period, I began reading descriptive accounts and novels related to Black history, as well as books about white fragility and privilege (see a bibliography in the appendix section). Among several others, I would highly recommend *The Warmth of Other Suns* by Isabel Wilkerson, three true stories associated with the Black "Great Migration." It takes place from 1910-1970, when millions of Blacks moved from the South to the North to escape Jim Crow laws, lynching, and other atrocities. I consider it a primer of sorts, not only based on its relatively recent history but also for gaining an understanding as to the depths of Black resiliency in the pursuit of liberty and justice. Also, I participated in many social and racial justice initiatives, conferences, and seminars and continue to do so today in the form of Zoom meetings due to pandemic restrictions. I also led a two-session book review at our parish of Ta-Nehisi Coates' best-selling book, *Between the World and Me.*

Essentially, the combination of R/A and its SC program furthered my awareness and grounded me through reading, learning, and meeting new people of all colors. It provided the foundation for me to launch more actively into the fray of racial and social justice advocacy. But then, another thing happened that further accelerated my future participation in this work.

The evening of the 2016 election, I was still deciding whether to register for a ten-session program over the course of almost three months that was premised on Black history and spirituality. It was called "Education for Action to Address Racism Collaborative" and I was hesitant due to the time commitment. To be perfectly honest, I was more unsure as to the depth of my commitment to discover more about myself — and the sharing that would likely be required.

My white fragility was showing, at least in my own mind. I went to bed early that night, fearing the direction toward which the election results were heading, woke up early the next morning, and had those results confirmed. It was the signal that I had no choice but to register to improve my knowledge of Black history. I signed up, along with Sandy, and it was one of the best decisions I ever made.

What eventually was renamed the "Movement for Antiracist Ministry and Action" (MAMA) covered the almost 700-year history of racism through the so-called discovery of America. It touched upon the brutalities brought upon millions of indigenous peoples, focused primarily on the capture of African Blacks and the introduction of "chattel" slavery, and then the subsequent horrors that millions of Blacks faced for more than four centuries.

Approximately twenty-five people participated, split evenly between Black and white. The studies and discussions brought Sandy and me to tears at times and awakened us to the level of commitment required in engaging racial justice. I never knew the depths of this history and am forever grateful that I accepted the call.

I was asked at the closing session to provide an overview of what I learned from the program:

- I discovered that I did not have any understanding of centuries of both Black and Native American experience This was due primarily to my educational isolation from these subjects and that school curricula at all levels were premised on white orientation, since we "owned the pens" that wrote the history

- That the values of courage, bravery, resilience, persistence, and deep faith are abundantly present in the Black and Native experiences, and both are built on the foundation of strong spirituality. Just imagine what could be possible as a country if all of us were working together in unity. Loyalties must transcend our own race, tribe, and class in the spirit of "whatever you do to the least of my brothers (or sisters), you do onto me."

- That whites must take it upon themselves to understand racism, not to depend on Blacks or other POC to educate and train us, and to learn how to move towards becoming antiracist in thought, word, deed, and policy.

- I met a young, white, schoolteacher participant whom I discovered was a developing local expert on the history of racism and redlining in the Rochester area; some of his material is noted in the first chapter.

After the formal part of program ended, we continued with a smaller MAMA group of Black and white alumni to help in its ongoing call to action. This is where I got into some "good trouble," as the late Congressman John Lewis phrased it. Program participants were asked to provide recommendations on how to best move forward with the program itself, as well as define action steps from what we learned. I put my white career background into play and came up with what I thought was respectful input about process, direction, and action. However, it lit a fuse with one key Black leader, and in the subsequent e-mail exchange, he labeled me a racist.

This took me aback as my intentions were completely honorable in my own (white) mind. But it taught me some key lessons in humility, to authentically listen, and to let others more experienced lead. I thought I was doing that, but if you were Black and burdened with 400 years of whites having louder voices, I can understand.

This may have been the most important lesson from my involvement with MAMA. The leader and I eventually reconciled and are friends to this day.

The action steps we developed led me to involvement with the aftermath of the "Take It Down" (TID) initiative and the Faith Community Alliance Coalition. TID was instrumental in getting the "pickaninny" art removed from the carousel at Rochester's Charlotte Beach and then became part of a mobile, historical art exhibit on Black history coordinated by the Rochester Museum and Science Center. Through these involvements, I was becoming increasingly attracted to issues within the city and informed in many ways, especially regarding poverty, the complex Rochester City School District (RCSD) situation going back decades, and the local Black experience of racial injustice within education. This led to an ongoing education on the issues associated with the RCSD and racism.

This takes me to late 2017, when Sandy and I assisted in coordinating a speaking event with Debbie Irving, author of *Waking Up White*. Over 100 people attended to learn about her "jolting and continuing journey from white oblivion to white awareness described in an honest way that may inspire others to do such transformational work on themselves" (Peggy McIntosh). Her story parallels my own, but with more eloquence.

Through 2018, I continued to be active in broadening my understanding of racism, but not yet pursuing any specific action such as antiracism advocacy. However, one important step Sandy and I took was to establish the Wynne-Strauss Fund for Social and Racial Justice with the Rochester Area Community Foundation. Our first grant from this fund went to the future creation of a new Civil Rights Park in Rochester.

Moving to Action

In early 2020, I was asked by a very good friend, colleague, mentor, and a fellow McQuaid alumnus to write a post about my racial and justice journey for his blog, "A White Guy in Rochester." He knew about my work during 2019, especially in the village of Fairport in the town of Perinton, where we lived. The following is an updated version of what I wrote:

      I was honored to be asked to be a guest contributor for

132

Frank Staropoli's blog and share my story of racial justice advocacy, as well as provide suggestions about addressing issues of structural and institutional racism head-on, especially through direct engagement with suburban power structures.

- My journey was not charted out as to where the currents might take me since I retired
- Over time, I kept coming back to two thoughts: grow where you're rooted and the power of personal relationships through encounter and dialogue with "others" i.e., BIPOC
- Also, one question that I heard routinely was "But what can one person do?" But was this a real question or an excuse to remain frozen and not to act?
- Early last year there was an awakening moment when I was challenged by a good, better-informed friend to take the next step with what I've learned and experienced. Whatever that next step was, I didn't know. My friend sensed that, based on my overall experiences, that I was well positioned to accept and move on his challenge.
- Overnight, I was inspired to explore what the Rochester Chamber of Commerce was doing to become more engaged with the Rochester City School District (RCSD) situation. I advocated for more active Chamber involvement with their president and a key board member as well as with our NYS Legislators.
- About the same time, I became familiar with the United States Catholic Bishops' 2018 letter against racism ("Open Wide Our Hearts: The Enduring call to Love") and participated in two related programs.
- I then proposed an educational program based on the Bishops' letter to our pastor of the Churches of Assumption and Resurrection (COTA-COR).
- He approved the proposal, and I developed a custom, seven-session, racial justice program foundational to learning more about personal and institutional racism, including within the Catholic Church.
- We had approximately forty people attend each session, and the plan then was to broaden community partic-

133

ipation and move beyond education to individual commitment and action. I presented a follow-up report to the Parish Council, outlining the specific action recommendations.

• One of these was to do a second "Sacred Conversations" program in early 2020, which I would co-facilitate.

• In November 2019, there were two Democrat & Chronicle articles titled "Suburbs Add to RCSD Burden" and "Unwanted?" alleging that suburban school districts were "dumping" vulnerable students into the RCSD; I took this as one more call to action.

• I subsequently met with the Fairport Central School District (FCSD) Superintendent and made public comments, asked questions, and offered suggestions at three subsequent FCSD Board meetings regarding the articles.

• I provided the board a presentation titled "The History of Segregation, Discrimination, and Racist Policy in Greater Rochester." This is a powerful presentation created by a Rush Henrietta teacher that has potential as both a learning tool for students and being instructive on the history of redlining and its impact on housing in our region. I indicated to the board that I could assist in coordinating a presentation.

• I also submitted a FOIA (Freedom of Information Act) request that revealed that the FCSD had in fact sixty-two movements of students to the RCSD over the past three years, more than two-thirds of which involved minorities.

• The FCSD continued to maintain silence on this issue, so I began participating in one of its own internal programs on raising racism awareness within the district.

• I planned on continuing to pursue this issue with the FCSD and brought it to the attention of both the Perinton and Village Boards as well as others.

• I took this step due to Frank's challenge in his recent blog titled the "Racial Divide" encouraging direct engagement with public officials.

• I encouraged them to attend an upcoming Sacred Conversations (SC) program.

• Here are my suggestions for the transformation of moving from "What Can One Person Do?" to "What One

Person CAN Do!" Be alert to the markers on your journey e.g., my (white) friend's encouragement that I was prepared to harness and act upon what I have already learned and experienced.

- Listen carefully to what your Black friends are telling you; do more listening than talking and don't depend on them for your own responsibility to "step out;" Let the "flow" of your experiences lead you naturally.

- Don't get bogged down by the quest for perfect information; if you do, consider it an excuse not to act!

- Take action step(s) and don't worry about making a mistake.

- Remember that awareness without action is not sufficient.

- One thing can lead to another as you can see, based on my journey over the past six years; just follow and connect the dots!

- Be intentional and accountable; I repeat: BE INTENTIONAL AND ACCOUNTABLE!

- Do not be afraid to be called a racist; I have had that experience and believe as whites we are ALL racist to one degree or another.

- Remember that "Few are guilty, but all are responsible." (Rabbi Abraham Joshua Heschel)

- A cautionary note: as Frank will tell you, this work has personal cost associated with it. Be prepared that some of those close to you may react in ways that might be surprising.

- Go forward with courage; my model for this is the incredible Black resilience of over 400 years in the face of the oppression, violence, and injustice they continue to endure, as outlined in MLK's famous letter from the Birmingham jail.

- Read Ibrahm X. Kendi's *How to Be an Antiracist.*

- Per Kendi, "a RACIST is one who is supporting a racist policy through their actions or inaction or expressing a racist idea. An ANTIRACIST is one who supports an antiracist policy through their actions or expressing an antiracist idea. Bottom line, to be an antiracist is a radical choice in the face of history requiring a radical reorientation of our consciousness." This is where I personally want to be, otherwise I risk being labeled a racist (although that would not be the first time as I indicated previously!). Reading *How to Be an Antiracist* is highly recommended but I wouldn't read this first if you are just starting out on your own path of re-learning and discovery.

• Realize that a policy change today could be insidiously or overtly reversed in the future; therefore, it is important to remain alert and steadfast on your antiracism journey.

• "Injustice anywhere is a threat to justice everywhere." (MLK)

This describes my racial and social justice path after 2010 and how I was led to participation and action. A developmental thread began with SC, followed by MAMA, and led to engagement with the TID Committee. Taking the next step eventually got me to the point where I had the background, fortitude, and skill to take some independent antiracism steps, such as I did with the FCSD.

Another less obvious blessing I received right from the start was an appreciation for Black Christian spirituality and all its resonate richness. Little did I know what was about to happen in 2020 that further developed my antiracism participation and advocacy, giving me an even deeper appreciation of the depth, endurance, and resilience of Black spirituality.

Illustrative of this journey, I want to repeat the note contained in the Preface that I sent to some of my relatives last year:

My overall (racial and social justice) journey, similar to my Camino walk, has been remarkable in terms of its interconnectedness, growth, and broadening my view of the world especially over the past six years. I have moved beyond a lot of my white fragility to better understand how white supremacy and privilege obstructed what I learned in K-16 about truly "Loving Thy Neighbor" or the "others." And I feel blessed to be able to share these thoughts of my journey with you in what, believe it or not, is an abbreviated testimony ... the beauty of which continues to grow including even providing this brief overview. I believe this is how a conversation could begin i.e., with open, honest dialogue where questions can be raised, responses given based on experiences, and with little or no preaching ... at least with words as St. Francis would often say! I hope you each feel the same way.

Unfortunately, conversations never happened but I did receive some ad hominem responses; however, I did not take these derogatory words to heart, as they cannot even come close to what Blacks have endured for centuries. As mentioned in the previous blog post, Black resilience has inspired me to carry on, irrespective of the personal price to be paid at times. It has also provided me a model for being resolute and to continue down this path.

Lastly, what words of advice would I give today to myself at the conclusion of this decade? Even though I finally discovered my voice and the beginnings of overcoming my complicit silence on racial injustice since 2014, I am very conscious of trying not to be deluded by any newfound self-righteousness. The path I am on continues within a complex mix of blessings, risks, and personal costs. Seeds of discontent continue to be sown in this country, widely dispersed and bearing deadly fruit. For me, the hopeful side of this lies within the more than four-hundred years of the Black and indigenous experience of resilience, persistence, and movement towards justice and equality.

Chapter 8
2020s: The Good, The Bad, and The Ugly

PIXABAY

The world has been dealing with the COVID-19 pandemic since March 2020.

"Do not look to the institutions to defend you – you must defend the institutions." (Timothy Snyder)

"The spiritual nature of a person's life is measured by love." (Pope Francis, 'Fratelli Tutti,' para. 92)

"Hope has two beautiful daughters; their names are Anger and Courage. Anger at the way things are and Courage to see that they do not remain as they are." (St. Augustine)

PEOPLE AND EVENTS IN THE NEWS, The 2020s: Daniel Prude, George Floyd, Jacob Blake, Breanna Taylor, Ahmaud Aubery, and the 4,000+ who preceded them via lynching and police related killings, Minneapolis, Kenosha, BLM protests, WHO, Wuhan, pandemic, COVID-19, millions of related deaths and disproportionate impact on POC, "essential workers," Fauci, Vaccine, Masks, Quarantine, Lockdown, Social Distancing, Distance Learning, Zoom, "Bubble," Recession, Jobs, unemployment, evictions, Impeachments, elections, Biden/Harris, Georgia, the "Big Lie," Capitol Insurrection, white supremacy, Bishop William Barber, Australian brushfires, California wildfires, Stock Market, Beirut, RBG, cybersecurity, Paris Climate Accord, carnage, Will/Brooks/Gerson/Steele, pepper spray of a nine-year old Black child, YHWH, OFW - $15/hr., rescue package, "Social Dilemma," Tyshon Jones, Daunte Wright, Lynn Cheney

In my lifetime and likely all others' born post-WWII who are still alive, we have never had so many dramatic and consequential events crammed into one year such as those experienced in 2020 and on into 2021. The chapter title I chose just happens to be one of my all-time favorite movies and I thought provided an appropriate description as we began a new decade. There were also scores of pictures and timeline events to choose from for this chapter, and I wanted to demonstrate a more global view of the pandemic rather than merely focusing on our national pain. Tragically, over three million people have died worldwide due to the pandemic in the past year, and US deaths are about 20 percent of that total as of this writing.

I have purposely attempted to minimize politics in writing this memoir, and there are many compelling reasons to do so considering the current public affairs milieu. There are those who consider the pursuit of racial and social justice political, but I prefer to view it as scripturally premised. Both Old and New Testaments provide ample statements of speaking truth to power, but none more so than the crucifixion of Jesus. Even though this speaking leads to some hard work and challenges within political channels, I view it as a movement premised on seeking common ground for the common good of the United States and all its citizens.

As noted at the beginning of Chapter 3, whites have a special responsibility in speaking out and being involved. Our voices will resonate louder within the systemic power structure of the country and our lives are less at risk in so doing.

To add to this discussion, many in the Church continue to erroneously label work on behalf of justice as politics. This leads to justification for not supporting things like the Civil Rights Movement. However, Catholic social teaching and work for social justice is scripturally premised and often involves advocating for government actions (legislative, executive, and judicial) to change existing policies, create new policies, and to allocate public money for such. Therefore, it requires participating in our political system, which Pope Francis said is good and necessary as citizens and Christians (see his address to the US Congress during his 2015 visit).

As mentioned in the previous chapter, the Catholic Church has spoken up most recently with the 2018 United States Conference of Catholic Bishops' (USCCB) document on racism, "Open Wide Our Hearts: The Enduring Call to Love." Continuing the Church's social teaching mandate as rooted in scripture, this pastoral letter from the full body of bishops to Catholics and all people of goodwill addresses the evils of racism. It tasks each of us to remember that we are all brothers and sisters, equally made in the image of God.

In the latter part of the twentieth century, there were several similar letters and other calls from the bishops to the laity about racism. This brings about an important question of, although timely in terms of current events, how Catholics will authentically respond to the truths addressed in this most recent letter. I am currently pursuing this with the Diocese of Rochester, to see how the action steps called for in the letter will be addressed locally and with intentionality in a post-COVID mode. Based on the persistence of racism in this country, we cannot wait for another letter from the bishops twenty or thirty years from now.

I continued with my antiracism activities from 2019 through the pre-COVID period of 2020, I define as through March 15, roughly coinciding with the early stages of the national response to the pandemic. These included several follow-up discussions and presentations to the FCSD Board and superintendent, the Perinton Town Board, and the Fairport Village Board on the racial justice matters facing the community. Sandy and I also had to cancel our Civil Rights tour scheduled for Georgia and Alabama in March; that was an initial COVID disappointment but paled in comparison to all the subsequent circumstances people have had to endure since. During this period, I developed the course outline for the second Sacred

Conversations (SC) program at our parish, which quite coincidentally (and thankfully) concluded on March 14, when everything began to shut down.

Implementing this second SC program was an action step emanating out of the seven-week racism awareness program I coordinated in the fall of 2019 at our parish and built around the core curriculum of the first SC program we participated in 2016. In 2018, Sandy and I were both trained to be SC facilitators, but I hadn't facilitated any sessions until this one. I adapted the program to add a Fairport context, using my work associated with the FCSD as a case study on racism as well as other historical information, including a forgotten 1920 story of a tragic Fairport police killing of a young, unarmed Black.

The man's name was James Noey, and my SC co-facilitator, Rev. Wanda Wilson, discovered the incident which happened near where the Fairport Village Office is now located. The 100th anniversary of Mr. Noey's killing was October 2020 and through my encouragement, the *CITY* newspaper wrote a commemorative article about it. The relationship of this local incident to the police killings of 2020 100 years later cannot be understated.

In November 2019, I read two *Democrat and Chronicle* (D&C) articles alleging that suburban school districts were "dumping" vulnerable students into the Rochester school district. After gathering support from some other community members, I wrote a letter and later met with the Fairport Central School Board about my concerns.

Discussions with the school board regarding these matters were ongoing. You can read more about of these discussions in the Appendix. There, you'll find details on my submission of a Freedom of Information Act request to the FCSD regarding student transfers between 2016 and 2018 and the results of those findings, my attempt to get feedback from the board on these findings, and a promise by an FCSD policy committee member promising a full review of transfer policies and a follow up with me. Following that is a list of recommendations program participants at the Sacred Conversations on Race and Action session on March 14, 2020, made in an effort to foster effective antiracism actions.

Considering the challenging antiracism work from 2019 through the first quarter of 2020, I think this chapter is titled appropriately and demonstrates both the power and the potential of the Sacred Conversations program. The power is primarily in the relationships built and what both Black and white participants typically learn about each other within the context of the continued "stickiness" and tragedy of white supremacy-induced racism.

The potential is in what we now do about it, and to be perfectly blunt, this is mostly unrealized potential, at least on a collective basis whether at the parish level, diocesan, or within community organizations. Said another way, new and heightened awareness brought about by programs like SC must be actualized via individual and collective action, otherwise we will continue staring into the same racism abyss.

I learned a great deal about what being an authentic antiracist means from my co-facilitator, Rev. Wanda Wilson. She is a Black, female pastor of her own church, was one of the facilitators in our first SC program and was also one of the developers and facilitators of the MAMA program. Wanda would challenge me to go well beyond my white, embedded background and push me to a closer understanding of what antiracism is and what it is not. The emphasis is on going well beyond words and into action, with a special focus on systemic policy change and accountability for associated outcomes.

An additional blessing through our work together was to witness how tirelessly Rev. Wanda put her faith into action and how she encouraged me to do the same. I cannot speak to individual actions taken by program participants since, and the pandemic has surely limited our abilities to become more involved through the parish or other organizations. I periodically send out material to increasingly summon both the individual and collective will to do even more antiracism work, based on the white supremacy forces unleashed in 2020 and continuing into 2021.

I have been and will continue to follow-up on several of the action steps outlined previously, and I encourage any reader to choose just one of those listed, or one of their own, and hold themselves accountable to follow through via a monthly self-check.

As winter turned to spring, I continued to be involved with advocacy work, primarily with the FCSD. The district decided to begin immediate implementation of an antiracist curriculum I had previously recommended to them, and now most other suburban school districts are implementing the same curriculum. The importance of having this antiracism subject matter and associated teacher training in local public schools cannot be overstated.

Also, the Monroe County Council of School Superintendents jointly signed a Fight Against Racism Pledge in 2020. This appears to have been somewhat prompted by the combination of the George Floyd and Rayshard Brooks police killings in Minneapolis and Atlanta respectively around Memorial Day.

Shortly after these tragic incidents, I began to have discussions with leaders of the Fairport Black Lives Matter (BLM) movement. I offered assistance to help get BLM to the board tables of the three local government entities and, as mentioned in a previous chapter, I've also been participating in weekly, silent, peaceful BLM rallies coordinated by Elders and Allies, together with the Sisters of St. Joseph and the Sisters of Mercy.

I have also participated in countless Zoom conversations about a variety of local and national social and racial justice issues, including two I should mention. The first relates to a COTA-COR Task Force called Becoming A Beloved Community. It was created in the late summer to assess antiracism and the diversity context within the Fairport area to heighten social and racial justice awareness of parishioners and other community members. I participated on the task force and contributed my updated work with the FCSD. A twenty-five-page report was produced and made available to all parishioners via the parish website.

Included in the report were recommendations for more affordable housing in Fairport. I had previously been in conversation with Fairport's deputy mayor about increasing the inventory of affordable housing in the area, which is virtually nonexistent; I subsequently submitted input on this issue to both the village and town as part of the updates to their respective, ten-year strategic plans.

The second initiative relates to a diocesan proposal to shut down the historic St. Michael's church, located in an impoverished, primarily Hispanic/Latinx section of the city. I was asked by a priest friend from my St. Bonaventure days to participate in the initial, grass roots planning to save the facility. I provided some initial guidance and, as of this writing, the matter remains unresolved for a variety of reasons.

There is a need for more transparent articulation of the diocese's vision about city parishes, the communities they serve, and creative funding alternatives as needed. There could be some distraction on the part of diocesan officials brought about by the ongoing sexual abuse case, associated settlements, and the dwindling number of available priests. Unfortunately, the people who suffer are the city faithful among the most underserved and marginalized. This follows a similar pattern throughout the country.

Tragically, any discussion of the 2020s would not be complete without an overview of how I believe white supremacy has fully revealed itself and how it has contributed to arguably the four key 2020-2021 societal issues of the times: COVID, police brutality and protests, the 2020 elections and voter suppression, and the Capitol insurrection. Each of these has specific and deplorable racial characteristics such that "bad" and "ugly" are appropriate terms. Let's take them one at a time and examine how I perceive the intersection of white supremacy and institutional and systemic racism (please see the appendix for definitions).

Regarding COVID-19, the resulting deaths in this country and throughout the world continues to reach new heights. In the US, there were almost 600,000 deaths by the end of April 2021, roughly 20 percent of the world total, with hundreds of thousands more projected. This carnage is horrible enough, but the disproportional impact on Blacks is very disturbing, though not surprising given our country's racial track record. Blacks have two times the COVID death rate of whites while being only 13 percent of the country's population.

Even with vaccines now available, a similar disproportion prevails, with whites currently being vaccinated at a rate two to three times higher than Blacks. There are many, decades-old factors contributing to this tragic imbalance: these include higher rates of underlying health conditions; less access to care; Blacks holding many "essential" jobs; insufficient information; housing disparities, and many more.

The epidemic of police brutality was clearly visible via our ubiquitous technology and social media with the murder of George Floyd by a police officer in May 2020. It sparked what could be considered the largest protest movement in American history. There were several other police killings of young Blacks, their names listed at the beginning of this chapter. The resulting protests were widespread throughout the country and, although the vast majority were peaceful, there were many incidents of riots, destruction, looting, death, and thousands of protester and police injuries. It also led to a heightened awareness and engagement of the important BLM movement and discussions throughout the country on criminal justice and police reform.

Due to a massive upswing in police brutality on Blacks continuing in the spring of this year, even Pat Robertson spoke out. This ultra-conservative televangelist, political commentator, former Republican presidential candidate, and Southern Baptist minister said that cops have "got to stop this stuff." Of Derek Chauvin, the officer convicted of murdering George Floyd, Robertson said, "I mean, they oughta put him under the jail." There is hope with statements like this coming from well-known, white evangelicals; however, the systemic nature of police brutality must be intensely analyzed. It is not simply a matter of a "few bad apples," what Catholic officials sometimes label priests who commit sex abuse crimes on children.

Cities can appoint all the Black cops, Black chiefs, Black mayors, and Black district attorneys they want, but until leaders and reformers dig deeper into the systemic roots of racism, disproportionate killings and murders of young Blacks will continue. As the local D&C concludes in a April 25, 2021, editorial: "Until it is instilled in police that their first loyalty is to the George Floyds of the world, there will be no winners for the conviction of Derek Chauvin."

Let us take up the cause now, and I encourage readers, especially whites, to become familiar with the possibilities and engage where they see themselves best fitting in. As citizens and taxpayers, we cannot continue to use the police for a convenient safety and security cover and, in some cases, as the scapegoats of our own racism.

The 2020 elections, which resulted in the "Big Lie" and the associated, highly visible voter suppression tactics utilized in many states, continued what has been an ongoing, deliberate, and prevailing white supremacy movement for over 150 years. The 1965 Voting Rights Act is sometimes heralded as the corrective legislative step taken to eliminate primarily Black voter suppression. But, just as history has demonstrated the "one step forward, two steps backward"

146

tendency over the years with Civil War era Reconstruction, the 1954 Brown case, the 1960's Civil Rights Movement, and other attempts to correct this country's original sin of racism, voter suppression tactics are alive, well, and thriving within many states as of this writing.

We can again try to correct this sinister, anti-democratic movement that has the distinct intent to keep whites in political offices and Blacks out. Congress should now pass the John Lewis Voting Rights Advancement Act. "This would block voter purges, ensure easy access to early voting and, restore federal supervision of voting changes in states with a history of voter suppression," says Richard L. Hasen, a professor at the University of California, Irvine.

For readers who might want to refer to my statement of trying to minimize anything political, please allow me this suggestion in the spirit of being pro-democracy as well as racial and social justice oriented. Passing the act would demonstrate a considerable step forward towards the elimination of white supremacy; not taking this step suggests the exact opposite. I strongly encourage readers to advocate for the "John Lewis" legislation on its own merits, in his honor and memory as one of our greatest civil rights leaders.

Yet another high-water mark of hundreds of years of white supremacy was arguably reached on January 6, 2021, with the Capitol insurrection. Pick your verb, but it was stoked, fomented, provoked, and incited by then-President Trump, who wanted to remain in power after a legitimate election of landslide proportions decided he was out after one term. I leave it at that, but what is not debatable since it was broadcast live throughout the world was that there were hundreds of insurrectionists who stormed and entered the Capitol, backed by thousands of others outside, and that several people died as a result, including three police officers. Michelle Goldberg spoke to this lawlessness in the January 15, 2021, *New York Times*: "An animating irony of Trumpism — one common among authoritarians — is that it revels in lawlessness while glorifying law and order."

It is estimated that 80 percent of the insurrectionists were white males and one was shockingly depicted carrying the abhorrent, treasonous, pro-slavery, racist, anti-Semitic, white supremacist, Confederate flag. The insurrectionists chose their whiteness over democracy and the riot has made it impossible for white Americans to deny that we have a gigantic, painful problem. The juxtaposition of the insurrection with the previous summer's BLM and other "Floyd" protests has illuminated how dangerous white supremacy is in a way that the other protests did not.

But denial is already creeping into all four of these 2020-21 tragedies, as race scholar Ibram X. Kendi has said: "The heartbeat of racism is denial. The American creed of denial — 'I'm not a racist' — knows no political parties, no ideologies, no colors, no regions."

A quote that relates to both the election and the insurrection from author and historian Timothy Snyder in the *New York Times* is as follows:

> America will not survive the big lie just because a liar is separated from power. It will need a thoughtful repluralization of media and a commitment to facts as a public good. The racism structured into every aspect of the coup attempt is a call to heed our own history. Serious attention to the past helps us to see risks but also suggests future possibility. We cannot be a democratic republic if we tell lies about race, big or small. Democracy is not about minimizing the vote nor ignoring it, neither a matter of gaming nor of breaking a system, but of accepting the equality of others, heeding their voices, and counting their votes.

The last four years have increasingly demonstrated how institutionally fragile our democracy is and that there appears to be many among us who want to knock the crystal of democracy off the table. If some people believe the lies about election fraud and continue in a frenzied state of denial, they might believe anything. What is necessary is for the truth of our deeply embedded, white supremist culture to be revealed. President Biden has begun this conversation by using the term white supremacy in his inaugural address; this is a simple yet important start to truth and reconciliation.

The Sacred Conversations on Race (SC) program offers a relevant opportunity to explore white supremacy as related to the four issues I chose to highlight in this chapter. Due to the ongoing intensity of these and many other racial injustice issues, Roc/ACTS is contemplating updating its SC curriculum. I forwarded them some suggestions that can be found in the Appendix. They have also asked me to continue my role as a facilitator.

The relatively recent introduction of the SC program and its impact on my life begs a question related to my Catholic upbringing and life as a practicing Catholic: Given my Catholic background and experience, why did it take so long for me to begin to understand the causes of social and racial injustices in this country? Why isn't there more preaching from the pulpit to prick people's consciences about the ongoing atrocities perpetrated on BIPOC, such as the disproportional COVID impact, relentless police brutality, and numerous other issues? Is the Church's well-known social justice ethos actually taught at the Catholic elementary and high school levels today? Why aren't there more motivated, justice-oriented people among the laity?

I know I am not alone as a white Catholic with these questions, and no doubt similar questions prevail within other white faith communities. Upon personal reflection, being a Catholic primarily meant having a rich sacramental life, the opportunity to get a superb education (if your family had the income) and offered numerous participation opportunities to live your faith as I have throughout my childhood and adult life. Even after all this, I knew very little that was Catholic-oriented about social and racial justice, other than what I have cobbled together on my own the past several years. I am probably not alone.

The absence of Catholic social justice teaching, while at the same time growing up within the vacuum of my mostly white world, was detrimental. Thankfully, I gradually overcame my lack of awareness. This enlightenment has empowered me as a layperson to discover my voice, and influenced my relationship with God and my ongoing spiritual development.

Speaking truth to power requires courage and not falling into the trap of being limited by the convenient excuse, subterfuge, and hypocrisy that some issues are political and therefore should not be openly discussed or preached from the pulpit. It also requires that any "speaking" will more effectively resonate within the context of being a humble, listening spirit without demonstrating any contempt for someone's position or opinion.

It strikes me, however, despite this educational gap depicted in my story, just how many priests, nuns, and deacons have impacted my life so profoundly and provided guidance for me to remain on the path of pursuing justice for all. They include Fr. Thomas Merton, Fr. Tony Valente, Fr. Bob Werth, Fr. Richard Rohr, Fr. Dan Riley, Fr. Bryan Massingale, Rev. Myra Brown, Deacon John McDermott, Sr. Grace Miller, the many other Sisters of Mercy, Sisters of St. Joseph, a multitude of other Jesuits and Franciscans, and of course, Pope Francis. This provides me some hope for the future of the Church.

Despite the heroic efforts of these holy people, the Catholic social justice educational disparity endures. Even what has been promulgated as one of the Church's latest testimonies against racism in this country, namely the USCCB's 2018 letter, "Open Wide Our Hearts: The Enduring Call to Love, A Pastoral Letter Against Racism," is lacking. Per a March 2021 Zoom presentation at the Bernardin Center by the activist Black priest, Fr. Massingale, there is no mention in the bishops' letter of Black Lives Matter, white nationalism, white privilege, or anti-Black racism. White people are portrayed as merely "absent, passive, and even saviors but never as agents of racial injustice." Fr. Massingale continues to say that there is "muted rhetoric regarding police violence and white supremacy, yet it condemns violent attacks against police." That was the only time the word "condemn" was used by the bishops in their letter.

It's no surprise that, when the 2020 protests occurred after the police killing of George Floyd and other Blacks, Fr. Massingale stated that there was outright hostility toward the BLM movement from priestly pulpits across the country. Protesters were labeled as "thugs, maggots, parasites, Marxists" and many more horrible names. Once again, the Church missed an opportunity with its official teaching to assist in righting our country's and the Church's many racist wrongs going back centuries.

But there is still time to change course if the will is there, and I am pursuing this with the local Catholic diocese. Lay people, those of us Catholics and non-Catholics alike sitting in the pews or watching on Zoom, must take up the slack (the cross) and join our faith leaders in ridding us of the evil of racism within the grace of transformational love. The laity MUST step up their game because the clergy cannot do it alone. A final comment on the 2020s: I cannot overstate the importance of how technology has introduced new possibilities of communicating in this era of social distancing. It is not the same as meeting for coffee, lunch, or a beer, but thankfully we have outlets like Zoom, Facetime, and more to keep important relationships connected and establish new ones. As one example, my "Rohr" group has been sustained via Zoom and has evolved into a small faith community of its own.

What words of advice do I have for myself moving forward? The almost 250-year experiment called the United States of America is under attack from within. Protected from external threats for the most part by two vast oceans, we once again are faced with confronting our own internal white demons as we did in the Civil War 160 years ago. The term "United" in the country's name is an oxymoron. It does not describe us at all and hasn't for years, with a divide as deep as the San Andreas fault but far more visible along racist lines.

The USA is "exceptional" in many ways, but some view this term as duplicitous and self-serving within our centuries-old, inglorious history of white supremacy and racial injustice. The cruelties that led to the Civil War were at the root of the "Big Lie," the Capitol insurrection, voting suppression legislation, COVID death inequities and the related vaccine rollout, police brutality, and much more. We must face up to the fact that we are not as exceptional as we think and must move in a new direction of truth and reconciliation.

One thing I consistently reflect upon and pray about is that both as a citizen of this country and a lay Catholic, I must continue to expand my voice courageously and within love for others. As the quote from Pope Francis' encyclical states: "the spiritual nature of a person's life is measured by love." Amen.

I want to conclude with a dialogue our daughter had with her eleven-year-old son, our oldest grandchild, last summer. Jack asked her what she thought was worse, COVID or racism, and in her wisdom, she flipped the question back to him. His response went something like this: "I think racism is worse because there is not a vaccine for it like there will be for COVID." How remarkable is that? In my mind, this offers considerable hope for his generation and others to follow. The older generations like mine have not yet discovered the vaccine for racism. Perhaps Jack's will.

One last note: Based on the variety and complexity of topics in this chapter, I would encourage you to reread Thomas Merton's call for racial justice described at the beginning of the Preface. That was written almost sixty years ago and is even more relevant today.

Chapter 9
Truth, Reconciliation, Hope, and Action

PIXABAY

"We can't always see the ways trees are in relationship because their complex world of roots lives underground. We, the human family, are also inextricably interconnected." - Richard Rohr, CAC

"The Nazis had succeeded in turning the legal order on its head, making the wrong and the malevolent the foundation of a new 'righteousness.' In the Third Reich evil lost its distinctive characteristic by which most people had until then recognized it. The Nazis redefined it as a civil norm ... Within this upside-down world Eichmann ... seemed not to have been aware of having done evil." (A Report on the Banality of Evil, Amos Elon)

"White supremacy is not the elephant in the room. It is the room." (Nelba Márquez-Greene, LMFT)

"I really only love God as much as I love the person I love the least." (Dorothy Day)

There is abundant power in the fine art of storytelling. What I mean by that is not in a fictional or mythical sense, but stories such as this memoir, which are premised on the *truths* of one's own personal experience and history. With that in mind, for this concluding chapter I have chosen two books that are both personal and historical that touch upon the genesis of white supremacy. The prior chapter revealed the modern manifestations and horrors of white supremacy. Why do most whites prefer to avoid discussing white supremacy's multifaceted grasp on our hearts, minds, and souls, such as I did when I first started writing this book?

Before I get into an overview of the books, I want to pause and say that white supremacy ravages all BIPOC and not just Blacks. The "I" (Indigenous) part of the term represents our Native American brothers and sisters who are also part of our inglorious racist history, and together with Blacks were the most severely impacted segment of our overall BIPOC population even before 1492.

The first book I want to discuss is entitled *Unsettling Truths – The Ongoing Dehumanizing Legacy of the Doctrine of Discovery*, written in 2019 by Mark Charles and Dr. Soong-Chah Ran. As the book cover describes, in its "prophetic blend of history, theology, and cultural commentary it reveals the far-reaching, damaging effects of the 'Doctrine of Discovery' (DoD)." An explanation of the many "unsettling" ramifications of the little-known fifteenth-century DoD (if I am any example) is in the following brief synopsis.

• The "Doctrine of Discovery" is a set of legal principles that governed the European colonizing powers, particularly regarding the administration of indigenous lands. It emerged from a series of fifteenth-century papal bulls, which are official decrees of the Catholic pope. The first of these bulls was issued by Pope Nicholas V on June 18, 1452.

• It granted permission to the king of Portugal "to invade, search out, capture, vanquish, and subdue Muslims and pagans ... to reduce their persons to perpetual slavery ... and to convert them to his and their use and profit." It could be argued that June 18, 1452, is the birthday of what today is labeled as white supremacy.

• However, we must go back even centuries earlier, when the final vestiges of the Roman Empire converted to the Christian Empire, or Christendom, when the true seeds were sown by the Roman

154

Emperor Constantine. In AD 325, Constantine called the Council of Nicaea, which produced the Nicene Creed.

• Forces and narratives at the time in effect named Constantine as "God's chosen ruler." However, as the book states, "The idea of Christendom, an earthly Christian empire, is an extra-biblical concept that is not aligned with the teachings of Jesus."

• This is important because of the theories that then began to surface due to the power conferred onto Christendom such as "exceptionalism," "triumphalism," and "just war theory" (see definitions in the Appendix).

• Centuries later, these manufactured theories and others led to "the problem with the DoD ... establishing the false notion of a more ethnically pure, European Christian supremacy, and today it furthers the mythology of American exceptionalism, which is rooted in the blatant lie of a white racial supremacy."

There is much more historical background on these topics, but let me move to the book's discussion on how the DoD influenced the more well-known and later concept of Manifest Destiny.

• "John L. O'Sullivan, editor of the 'United States Magazine and Democratic Review' coined the phrase 'Manifest Destiny' (MD) in 1845... He used the term to explain God's unique mission for America." It "reflected the belief that this young nation has the God-given right to rule the entirety of the North American continent."

• "The DoD had encouraged the conquest of a lesser people by a greater people. Therefore, the exceptional Anglo-Saxon people of the thirteen colonies would need to expand their influence and power."

• The book goes on: "America saw itself as a bulwark of Western civilization centered on belief in God ... and in the twenty-first century, most Americans continue to believe that their nation is indispensable and exceptional. While MD does not directly reference the papal bulls of the fifteenth-century Catholic church, the understanding of chosen-ness and the legacy of promised lands align closely with the imagination and narrative of the DoD."

The concept of white supremacy goes back farther to the country's founding, as the authors state:

• "And thus the assumption of white supremacy as established by the DoD and the myth of Anglo-Saxon purity is evident in the founding documents of the United States." It goes on further to say, "The lie of white supremacy is embedded deeply in the diseased theological imagination of the American Christian mind and serves as a foundation for the destructive sin of racism."

• "This implicit bias of white supremacy can be seen even in the language that is used today. Many ... who are considered to be on the forefront of the racial dialogue frequently use the term white privilege. However, the word privilege suggests that the inequality that favors white people is actually a blessing which they must learn to share. The term white privilege perpetuates an implicit bias. Whiteness is neither a privilege nor a blessing to be shared, it is a diseased social construct that needs to be confronted."

These privileges include the following, as noted in a Buzzfeed article (October 27, 2013, titled "17 Deplorable Examples of White Privilege — and this isn't even the tip of the iceberg.") A compelling metaphor for each of the following privileges is to consider them as 'blood diamonds' i.e., the benefits reaped by the white beneficiaries of racial injustice. See the Appendix for more background on the original meaning of "blood diamonds."

1. Because of white privilege, you'll never have to worry about becoming the victim of law enforcement officers.

2. Thankfully, you'll never have to know what it feels like to see your teenage son's death being mocked.

3. Because of white privilege, you'll never have to inform your children of the harsh realities of systemic racism.

4. White privilege means you can be articulate and well-spoken without people being "surprised."

5. Because of white privilege, you'll never know what it's like to have the following statistic looming over your head; one-third of Black men will go to prison at least once in their lifetime.

6. You can dress and act however you'd like without being labeled a thug, low life, gangster, etc.

7. White privilege allows you to speak on any particular subject without being the sole representative for your entire race; it allows you to believe that all people of color think alike and share similar views.

8. White privilege means no one questions why you got that really great job; it's assumed you were just highly qualified.

9. White privilege means not having to worry about your hair, skin color, or cultural accessories as the reason you didn't get a job.

10. White privilege means you don't have to worry about being monitored in a store just because the hue of your skin is a bit darker than most.

11. Having white privilege means people will never label you a terrorist.

12. White privilege means not being affected by negative stereotypes that have been perpetuated and ingrained so deeply into American society that people believe them to be fact.

13. White privilege means you never have to explain why cultural appropriation (see Appendix) is a bad thing.

14. White privilege means not having to worry about being stopped and frisked.

15. If you benefit from white privilege, you'll never be told to "get over slavery."

16. White privilege means that you're never just your own person.

17. Benefiting from white privilege means you can walk the Earth unaware of your color.

Each of these points can be considered a "blood diamond," mined from white privilege. The aptly titled "Unsettling Truths" goes into detail about Native American history, Manifest Destiny, and how President Lincoln's related legacy might be different than most Americans realize.

Some other truth-telling is in the book *Caste — The Origins of Our Discontents,* written in 2020 by Pulitzer Prize winner Isabel Wilkerson. It is described as giving "a masterful portrait of an unseen phenomenon in America as she explores ... how America today and throughout its history has been shaped by a hidden caste system, a rigid hierarchy of human rankings." The following excerpts provide a brief idea on "an eye-opening story of people and history, and a reexamination of what lies under the surface of American life today."

• "A caste system is an artificial construction, a fixed and embedded ranking of human value that sets the presumed supremacy of one group against the presumed inferiority of other groups on the basis of ancestry and often immutable traits." Such a system "uses rigid, often arbitrary boundaries to keep the ranked groupings apart, distinct from one another in their assigned places."

• "Caste and race are neither synonymous nor mutually exclusive. They can and do coexist in the same culture and serve to reinforce each other. Race, in the United States, is the visible agent of the unseen force of caste. Caste is the bones, race the skin. Caste is fixed and rigid. Race is fluid and superficial, subject to periodic redefinition to meet the needs of the dominant caste in what is now the United States."

• Caste's "very invisibility is what gives it power and longevity. And though it may move in and out of consciousness, though it may flare and reassert itself in times of relative calm, it is an ever-present through line in the country's operation."

• In the initial years of Germany's Third Reich, the Nazis began "debating how to institutionalize racism in the Reich," wrote Yale historian James Whitman, "and they began asking how the Americans did it." Per another historian, Jonathon Spiro, "Hitler especially marveled at the American 'knack for maintaining an air of robust innocence in the wake of mass death'; i.e., through the American custom of lynching. The United States was not just a country with racism, Whitman, the legal scholar wrote, it was the leading racist jurisdiction --- so much so that even Nazi Germany looked to America for inspiration. Their overwhelming interest was in the "'classic example,' the United States of America."

• It goes on to say that the Weimar regime "underestimated (Hitler's) cunning and overestimated his base of support. At the height of their power at the polls, the Nazis never pulled the majority they coveted and drew only 38 percent of the vote in the country's last free and fair elections. The old guard did not foresee, or chose not to see, that his actual mission was to exploit the methods of democracy to destroy democracy."

• There is more in Wilkerson's discussion on how the Nazis used American racial norms and laws. Incredibly, the Nazis did not want to promote racial injustice to the extent the Americans were doing. She closes with the following: "While the Nazis praised 'the American commitment to legislating racial purity,' they could not abide
158

'the unforgiving hardness' under which 'an American man or woman who has even a drop of Negro blood in their veins counted as Blacks.' The one-drop rule was too harsh for the Nazis." I must be honest and say that this is intensely chilling and embarrassing as an American to think about.

• She makes a strong case for white trauma and the price whites are paying for maintaining this posture of caste superiority. "Thus, a caste system makes a captive of everyone within it. Just as the assumptions of inferiority weigh on those assigned to the bottom of the caste system, the assumptions of superiority can burden those at the top with unsustainable expectations of needing to be several rungs above, in charge at all times, at the center of things, to police those who might cut ahead of them, to resent the idea of underserving lower castes jumping the line and getting in front of those born to lead. Caste assumptions created devastation on both sides of the caste divide and have made for a less generous society overall."

Wilkerson's *Caste* contains more that is equally unsettling and I would highly recommend reading it, as well as Wilkerson's award-winning book *The Warmth of Other Suns*, which I referenced earlier.

Both *Unsettling* and *Caste* convey powerful historical truths and explore our white supremacist roots and their deadly impact on our country's past, present, and seemingly foreseeable future. They have both influenced me and provided tremendous insight into racial injustices, not only in this country but the world, as well as illuminated the effort that will be required to eradicate this cultural malaise. Can we bend the curve? Do we want to? Are our hearts and minds "gated," limiting our views on others and their realities? Do we have the will to turn despair into hope and hate into transformative love?

These questions lead me to comment on the power of some terms and labels that are sometimes expressed in certain ways to convey what one person might think is a "truth" about another person, either directly or indirectly, or perhaps to evoke an immediate reaction in an attempt to smear a person or group. I can speak from personal experience that this has happened to me, but my experience cannot compare to that of BIPOC.

These include the whole spectrum of political terms such as radical, protester, progressive, conservative, liberal, righty, lefty, fascist, socialist, communist, pro-lifer, pro-choicer, populist, nationalist, snowflake, etc. There are also available derivatives of these words that can create "false flags" if used improperly, such as ad hominem attacks.

A couple of years ago, a good friend of mine asked me if I thought I was more liberal now versus years ago and I responded that I think labels and terms like that are very limiting in describing someone. I have also had some of these terms, their caustic derivatives, and others directed to me by family members. There are of course other terms, such as extremist, terrorist, and anarchist, that extreme care must be taken in their use. These are more commonly used in a criminal context, as recently with the insurrectionists. I am getting into this because, if we are ever to cross the abyss of our divisions, this perhaps inherent human tendency to label someone or a group must be avoided or used very carefully if we want to make any headway towards reconciliation.

Unsettling concludes with two chapters on reconciliation emanating from the truths outlined in the book, therefore the terms "truth" and "reconciliation" are joined in a potent and hopeful way. There can be no reconciliation until certain truths are acknowledged; regarding white supremacy, the challenges in doing this are more than steep. This country's deep denial of the sins of slavery and Manifest Destiny are multigenerational and embedded in our national norms, laws, policing, and psyche.

The way out of this is through energetic discovery, awareness, and awakening, perhaps leading to some basic, initial acknowledgment, repudiation, and apology for the sins of our past, i.e., in the Catholic parlance, a confession grounded in authentic lament. Once this is accomplished, then possible next steps such as systemic policy change or reparations can be considered, again in the Catholic parlance, a penance with some teeth. Not until these steps are taken will forgiveness flow.

How could something like this ever begin? The authors of *Unsettling* conclude:

> The USA needs a national dialogue on race, gender, and class. A conversation on par with the Truth and Reconciliation Commissions that took place in South Africa, Rwanda, and Canada. It must be inclusive dialogue, not one that takes

place in specific silos. And the church must be involved. But because the American church has so broadly accepted the heresy of Christian empire and because the Western church wrote the DoD, the church is currently incapable of leading this dialogue. It can participate, but it cannot lead ... Our only path to healing is through lament and learning how to accept some very unsettling truths.

This last point about the role of the Western church is direct, harsh, and perhaps arguable, but it is an understandable indictment in light of its inglorious history. Perhaps now will be the time the Western church steps up and effectively participates in the dialogue that is so needed.

Wilkerson's *Caste* similarly says in her epilogue, "Our era calls for a public accounting of what caste has cost us, a Truth and Reconciliation Commission, so that every American can know the full history of our country, wrenching though it may be. You cannot solve anything that you do not admit exists, which could be why some people may not want to talk about it: it might get solved."When an accident of birth aligns with what is most valued in a given caste system, whether being able-bodied, male, white, or other traits in which we had no say, it gives that lottery winner a moral duty to develop empathy for those who must endure the indignities they themselves have been spared. It calls for a radical kind of empathy." She concludes: "A world without caste would set everyone free."

The natural flow of confession and penance then opens the door for forgiveness in "70 x 7" scriptural terms. As one of Richard Rohr's reflections suggests, "God has created a world where there is no technique or magical method for purity or perfection. Forgiving love is the only way out and the only final answer is God's infinite Love and our ability to endlessly draw upon it. Forgiveness is simply the religious word for letting go."

Once we get to this point, we can begin to work together in solidarity, which he says "... means much more than engaging in sporadic acts of generosity. It means thinking in terms of community. It means that the lives of all are prior to the appropriation of goods by a few. It also means combating the structural causes of poverty, inequality, the lack of work, land and housing, the denial of social and labor rights."

A good segue into now discussing hope is a connection back to the "Tony" chapter, as depicted in the laughing and spirited face of "Christ the Liberator." A liberator can be defined as a door or gateway, freeing people from bondage, encouraging the truth and hope, taking off our chains of bondage brought on by our sins of racism. I see liberation once experienced as then moving towards one of my aspirational goals as a "unifier," which takes me back to another chapter on "connecting the dots." Last year, one of the members of my "Rohr" group wrote me the following:

> Bill, you are a contemplative activist. As I read today's Rohr meditation, I thought of you throughout. "Their lives embody the beautiful struggle that is revealed when we seek to hold heaven and earth together through our love and faithfulness to God, humanity, and creation." Thanks for being light to the world! ... to be an expanding force, not a contracting force ... it does require lots of wisdom! But you have committed to the learning curve which is to be committed to following the guidance of the Spirit. Rock on!

I hope I can live up to his humbling words for the rest of my life.

Richard Rohr says, "The theological virtue of hope is the patient and trustful willingness to live without closure, without resolution, and still be content and even happy because our Satisfaction is now at another level, and our Source is beyond ourselves."

In his short book entitled, *Just This*, he adds "The virtue of hope, with great irony, is the fruit of a learned capacity to suffer wisely, calmly, and generously. The ego demands successes to survive; the soul needs only meaning to thrive. Somehow hope provides its own kind of meaning, in a most mysterious way."

As I look back on my life, my Camino walk provides a splendid metaphor for hope. During my daily walking regimen, I was continuously in a position of waiting (hoping) for the next yellow marker (usually an arrow) on the path to show me the way. Over the course of 500 miles, you did not want to miss one of these arrows, which on occasion did happen. I only had one really bad experience in going the wrong way that cost me a few hours. But on that one occasion,

I learned "to suffer wisely and calmly" for the most part and, amazingly, I connected with a French couple I had crossed paths with several times previously. I then began to walk with them the rest of the journey and we remain friends to this day.

The metaphor in this case was the markers that always brought me hope, just like the markers we experience every day in our lives that are sometimes invisible in the moment. When revealed, they possibly lead to unexpected experiences or new relationships that change our lives forever.

Another example of how this has worked itself into my life is the reference above by my fellow Rohrian brother suggesting that I am a "contemplative activist." I did not even know the meaning of this term just a few short years ago, and it is at the essence of the Rohr contemplation and action philosophy/movement. What happened was a product of having a conversation in a bar with a couple of Bonaventure friends that led to discovering who Richard Rohr was, as well as eventually starting our small discussion group. This has been a continuing, life-changing experience brought about through hope as "the patient and trustful willingness to live without closure and resolution," as described above by Richard Rohr. I was essentially being called while at the same time open to discovering new possibilities within my developing spiritual journey.

Understanding Rohr's Order, Disorder, Reorder cycle I believe unveils and illuminates hope when darkness appears in our lives, such as the events of 2020-2021 did to most of us. In the CAC's (Rohr's New Mexico based organization) latest Mendicant publication, it says:

> The pandemic joined forces with other pandemics, such as racism, poverty, and climate change. This time of disorder has ripped off the band-aid of denial. Once we see, we can't not see. But it's not only the difficult truths that are being unveiled; it's also the hopeful ones.
>
> Yet the disorder of our current time is nevertheless pregnant with the ever-emerging truth of reorder. Our primary task is to receive and trust the hope and promise that God offers us in these times, and all times. Such a posture does not absolve us of committed action and collective problem-solving, but rather aligns our intent and impact.

The last sentence serves to introduce my personal commitments to action either new or already in motion. These are also possibilities for readers to consider acting upon. As my Rohr group understands, as well as some other friends, I am more inclined to emphasize the "action" part of being a "contemplative activist" and utilize my daily three-to-four-mile walks for contemplation; during these walks, synergistically and in somewhat "mysterious ways," possible actions pop into mind.

So, as I come to a close, the following commitments are made in the spirit of what one person *can* do.

• Meet individually with anyone who would like to discuss this memoir in more depth and hopefully share their stories, experiences, and differences of opinion as well; and most importantly, within the discipline of deep listening (see https://www.youtube.com/watch?v=lyUxYflkhzo) and probing questions.

• Similarly, I also offer doing small group book review sessions with a special focus on youth and young adults — our future and greatest hope — and listen to their stories as well. The ongoing struggle in revealing the sins of white supremacy is going to require younger blood with passion, creativity, and keen listening skills to reimagine Dr. Martin Luther King's "Beloved Community."

• As an ally, continue my advocacy for local BLM initiatives, including those sponsored by the local and growing group, Elders and Allies, as well as Roc/ACTS with a special focus on moving towards modeling "truth and reconciliation" on a local basis. A related question inspires my advocacy: what does it say about us that the declaration "Black Lives Matter" is controversial?

• Support and advocate for the national Poor People's Campaign (PPC) led by Rev. Dr. William Barber, who recently said: "Where does healing come? What doesn't heal us is conversations about left versus right. The way to heal the soul of the nation is to pass policies that heal the body of the nation. It's the just thing to do. That's how we as a nation can together move forward." There are not many groups that bring ALL the poor, whether BIPOC or whites, together in mutual hope like the PPC does. Its advocacy for "One Fair Wage" of $15/hour "raises all boats," especially the 62 million Americans who do not have a living wage.

• Use my voice in speaking truth to power to fight white supremacy via continued local antiracism advocacy; this likely will be one of the most challenging commitments, especially related to the local diocese's seemingly faux interest — and in some cases back-peddling — regarding antiracism initiatives, as well as participation with the broadening local conversation on Police Accountability and Reform.

• More active engagement with the Spiritus Christi faith community, located in the city and led by a highly spirited, Black female priest. I am sadly disappointed with the local Catholic diocese for not being at the forefront of combating racism with a robust diocesan-wide antiracism agenda despite at least three National Bishops' Conference letters on racism over the past several decades.

• In the face of this disillusionment, I am currently collaborating with several diocesan parish representatives in moving towards becoming fully inclusive antiracist communities. I believe that the only way this can be accomplished is with a spiritual conversion of heart (metanoia). This parallels a December 12, 2020, Rohr reflection: "It is not mystical experience we are after but radical interior transformation, so that others may experience Christ more fully in us." Any such change must incorporate acknowledgment of white supremacy and white privilege as dominating factors within society, as well as the Church, and determine specific community steps for change. Laypeople must step up to this challenge and put aside our complicit silence within a sense of justice and compassion. For those of us who are Catholic, let's demonstrate who we really are!

• Although I do not necessarily think of reading books as a strong antiracism action, in the coming months I am going to finish reading Pope Francis' latest encyclical, *Fratelli Tutti, on Fraternity and Social Friendship*. It is an important contribution to the Catholic Church's rich tradition of social doctrine and must be preached widely.

• Continue to engage with Fairport school officials and local government leaders on antiracism initiatives, including related school policies, broadening the FCSD curriculum regarding our racial history, affordable housing, updated village police policies per state mandate, and others. I recently met with the Village of Fairport Board and mayor about policing issues. A footnote worthy of mentioning: I was recently rewarded by my granddaughter in association with my efforts to introduce the racial history curriculum into Fairport schools. This rich, complex history has recently been launched in the district and she informed me that her fourth-grade class has started studying racism.

• Additionally, I will be monitoring the incorporation of this racial history into local Catholic schools and am proud to say that Mc-Quaid Jesuit is currently assessing how they might implement the full curriculum. McQuaid would be the first local Catholic school to do this, as far as I know.

• Ongoing development and broadening of my Black relationships through authentic listening to their stories and experiences. This will contribute to my ongoing transformation, reinforced by the always present ODR cycle of life. To me, these relationships are the precious benefits of diversity and the true "diamonds."

• Be a model for the principles of subsidiarity and solidarity. Subsidiarity is the idea that a central authority should have a subsidiary function, performing only those tasks which cannot be performed effectively at a more immediate or local level. Solidarity is an awareness of shared interests, objectives, standards, and sympathies creating a psychological sense of unity of groups or classes.

• Fully inform our children and, at some point, our grandchildren on the social and racial justice fund, the Wynne-Strauss Fund for Social and Racial Justice that Sandy and I established in 2018 with the Rochester Area Community Foundation. We are grateful that we have been able to provide several small grants to local non-profits, including two for the creation of a planned Civil Rights Park in Rochester. Another grant was made to Boston University's Center for Antiracist Research directed by Ibram X. Kendi. After we pass, our children, and then our grandchildren, will become administrators of the fund. This is part of our legacy as full family partners on helping to dissolve social and racial injustices for decades to come. Any proceeds generated by sales of this book will be directed to this fund.

• I offer an open invitation to anyone interested to sit in on our Rohr group Zoom discussions, held about twice a month. We are a faith community of our own and perhaps a model for others to consider and to learn more about Fr. Richard Rohr, the CAC and, most importantly, themselves. Based on my own personal experience with my fellow Rohrians, I can attest to my own spiritual growth and development. The informal, relaxed environment has allowed me to share doubts about my faith, discuss my spiritual life, and to be comfortable in being vulnerable with others. A new member to the group recently mentioned how impressed and surprised he was to see these practices in action with his own eyes.

• I will be closely monitoring two developing movements. One is the locally based "Inclusive Recovery" and the second is "Solidarity Dividends," referenced by Heather McGhee in the February 14, 2021, New York Times and in her recent book, *The Sum of Us.* They both relate to a vision of prosperity and social improvements across racial lines for all people. Worthy of note is that, in a May,11, 2021, presentation of the Rochester Area Community Foundation, ACT Rochester, and the Washington, D.C.-based Urban Institute, it was stated that the Greater Rochester area remains one of the most highly segregated in the country. This decades-long issue represents a significant challenge to any "Inclusive Recovery" plan. I will be meeting soon with the two local presenters of that May program to discuss the ongoing development of this plan and a possible connection with both "Solidarity Dividends" and "Truth and Reconciliation."

• Continue my quest of being an advocate for seeking the common good and encourage other like-minded folks to do the same. Only in so doing will we hopefully move closer to our national destiny of becoming "a more perfect union."

• Lastly, use the many unearned privileges I have been blessed with towards the pursuit of broadening the privilege context within ALL "others" lives.

• Ms. McGhee in her book also references another significant national model I will be discussing titled "Truth, Racial Healing and Transformation" (TRHT) developed by the US TRHT Commission. She quotes in her notes "TRHT is a national effort and throughout the next two to five years there will be place-based TRHT processes in 14 communities including: the State of Alaska; Baton Rouge and New Orleans, Louisiana, Buffalo, New York; Chicago, Illinois; Dallas, Texas; Los Angeles, California; Richmond, Virginia; Selma, Alabama; Saint Paul, Minnesota; and Battle Creek, Flint, Kalamazoo, and Lansing, Michigan." She goes on to explain in her book that the word "reconciliation" was intentionally left out by the Commission and she quotes the Commission as follows: "To reconcile ... connotes restoration of friendly relations — 'reuniting' or 'bringing together after conflict' [whereas] the US needs transformation. The nation was conceived ... on this belief in racial hierarchy."

I hope you will consider joining me on this antiracism journey, no matter whether starting from a place of comfort or, preferably, discomfort as that is where the learning and transformation can truly ignite. My prayer is that perhaps my story, with all its stumbles along the way, can help answer the question of "What can one person do?" and drive one from being stuck or frozen to becoming more involved and work towards effective antiracism.

Like the "arrows" on our path or stars in the sky, taking action steps like the above might provide guidance, illumination, awakening opportunities, and epiphanies that we cannot begin to imagine due to the blanket of whiteness all around us.

The fulfillment of BIPOC and white balance in our world would mean that the tragic, pernicious plague of white supremacy would be finally eliminated. But that is going to take each of us as broken, "Holy Fools for Christ" to forcefully reveal and fight the insanity of racism.

My personal view of white privilege as created out of white supremacy, especially white MALE supremacy, is that it encumbers all white people in this country to one degree or another, whether they are aware of it or not. For instance, asking myself the simple question of when I first realized I was white? True answer: I honestly do not know since my privilege never allowed it to surface. If you are white, please take a moment to ponder that question for yourself. Related questions include: once you become conscious of this new reality, what comes next i.e., is there a possible pursuit of continuing learning and discovery that could be considered? How will the courage be found to do this and then move to speaking truth to power? How can one become more open and vulnerable to even ask these and other questions?

In closing, I offer this reading from author James Baldwin's *Nobody Knows My Name*, written in the early sixties. It was recited at a Black Lives Matter Memorial I attended in October 2020, with about 150 others at Highland Park, where thirty-one Black and Latinx names, killed at the hands of police, were read aloud.

Any real change implies the breakup of the world as one has always known it, the loss of all that gave one an identity, the end of safety. And at such a moment, unable to see and not daring to imagine what the future will now bring forth, one clings to what one knew, or dreamed that one possessed. Yet, it is only when a man is able, without bitterness or self-pity, to surrender a dream he has long possessed that he is set free — he has set himself free — for higher dreams, for greater privileges.

This defines what St. Paul meant by a "Holy Fool" for Christ. I could not have ended this book with a more appropriate passage. Peace and Godspeed!

Afterword

JEFF KELLOGG

Hudson River at North River, New York, where the author has requested his ashes be placed.

"The river is everywhere. They listened silently to the water, which to them was not just water, but the voice of life, the voice of Being, the voice of perpetual Becoming." (Siddhartha, Hesse)

"There is a balm in Gilead, to make the spirit whole. There is a balm in Gilead, to heal the sin-sick soul." ("There Is a Balm in Gilead," Negro Spiritual)

"May all of the stones covering up the openings to our tombs be rolled away." (Claude Adair)

" ... I have come to see that [there] must be a massive movement organizing poor people in this country, to demand their rights at the seat of government in Washington, D.C. ... and by that I mean all poor people ... And for those who will not allow their prejudice to cause them to blindly support their oppressor, we're going to have Appalachian whites with us in Washington." (Rev. Dr. Martin Luther King Jr., March 10, 1968, "The Other America").

We Have Never Been More United

A post on January 24, 2021, by James Mulholland, a sixty-year-old white man and father of a thirteen-year-old Black daughter, on his blog, "Note to My White Self," reflecting on his latent racism and white privilege, says the following:

I am tired of white people complaining that our nation "has never been so divided." This complaint is more evidence that white people are ignorant of our history and of their privilege. We are a nation that once fought a bloody civil war over whether we could enslave Black people. What the insurrection at the Capitol revealed was not something new, but an ugly and racist division that has been sustained since our nation's founding. When it comes to the work of creating a diverse and vibrant democracy, we have never been more united.

Consider this. In 1790, after the signing of the US Constitution, only property owning or tax paying white men could vote. White was defined as people of Anglo-Saxon origin. Women of all races and backgrounds, Blacks (free and enslaved), Irish, Italians, Hispanics, Chinese, Native Americans and many more were disenfranchised. This meant 6 percent of the population held power over the other 94 percent. When it comes to who holds power, our nation was never less democratic than in 1790.

It would not be until 1828 that the last U.S. state would eliminate property owning and tax paying requirements. For the first time, most white men could vote. Yet they still represented only about 35 percent of the US population. Sadly, this minority would enshrine their dominance across our culture, establishing white male supremacy as the guiding principle for church, government, family, and society. Those who disputed this inequity were ostracized, oppressed, imprisoned, and murdered. We were a democracy only if you were a white man.

That 80 percent of the insurrectionists at the Capitol were white men should not surprise us. Only white men could look at what has happened in our country over the past few decades and conclude we need a revolution. Only white men would see the presidency of Barack Obama as a threat. Only white men would celebrate the election of a white, narcissistic strongman. For many others, today's society is the evolution we have dreamed of – a multicultural nation where no gender, sexual orientation, race, or ethnic background is legally privileged.

The American story is not one of reclaiming some past glory, but of gradual empowerment. Over the decades since our nation's founding, the powerless have taken Jefferson's words as truth and repeatedly challenged white male supremacy. In 1869, the fourteenth Amendment gave the vote to all Black men. For a few short years, nearly 50 percent of our population was enfranchised. Black men served in the Senate and House of Representatives. For about eight years, racial equity looked like a possibility. Sadly, this splendid failure would be the high-water mark of our democracy for the next 100 years.

In the years after the Reconstruction, little progress was made, especially for people of color. In 1920, though all women received the vote, only white women were able to demand this right. Essentially, white women were invited into the all-male club with the unstated agreement that they continue to sustain white male supremacy. Together, this ugly alliance of white men and women fought the inclusion of everyone else.

It would not be until 1943 that people of Chinese descent were granted the vote. Until 1957, many states still denied the vote to Native Americans. Until the Voting Rights Act of 1965, most Blacks could not access the voting booth. Even after that Act, white legislators in state after state did all in their power to obstruct minorities from voting.

If a democracy is a government of "all the people," the United States is a young democracy. Only in the last few years has most of our adult population had access to the vote. Only in the last few years have white men and women realized their 250 years of national dominance is in danger. Only in the last few years have white men and women cared about the historic divisions in our nation – divisions that were previously to their advantage. Ironically, those who invaded our Capitol claimed to be patriots defending democracy. In actuality, they were insurrectionists trying to topple it.

Here is the good news of today.

Q&A with the Author

In the Preface, I referenced three, open-ended questions forwarded to family members in the summer of 2020. They go as follows, with my own personal responses.

Q What are your stories and reflections of growing up and continuing to live as a white person in a city, county, state, country, and world with so much and increasing diversity?

A This book has provided most of the important stories of my "growing up white" years and into the present day. The rest of my life I envision following through on the actions I committed to in Chapter 9, with a special focus on sharing my story in conversations with others. I am also considering writing about new, personal racial justice discoveries and relationships in whatever a post-COVID world might offer, and perhaps include insights from my four grandchildren.

***

Q What do you wish for your children, grandchildren, nieces, nephews, friends in this ever-changing, diverse world?

A The younger generations are the true hope for this country, especially those still in school as they continue to reimagine what the world can be. I hope that our grandchildren take full advantage of the opportunities for discovery through active community participation resulting in diverse, mutually enriching relationships.

***

Q What legacy do you wish to leave that will help them navigate the future perhaps better than we have in our own lives?

A My hope is that there are examples in my life that provide each of them something foundational to build their own social and racial justice legacies for their grandchildren and others. The Wynne-Strauss Fund for Social and Racial Justice that Sandy and I created provides a connection with the remaining part of this century to contribute to the pursuit of justice for all. Then it will be up to our grandchildren's children to continue this work into the next century.

***

An added question and response:

Q Besides being an ally in solidarity with the local Blacks Live Matter (BLM) movement, why are you participating in the weekly BLM Saturday demonstrations?

A These demonstrations are basically peaceful, silent, nonviolent expressions of support for our Black brothers and sisters. Usually, there are about twelve to fifteen older whites, primarily female, including several nuns, holding signs and flags at frequently traveled road intersections for one hour. For me, it brings a great sense of satisfaction to participate in this relatively simple way and to hear all the people honking their horns in support of BLM. Occasionally there will be a shout back like, "All lives matter!" but at least some awareness has been raised. One person has a sign that says "All Lives Matter When Black Lives Matter" — the real message of BLM. I also look at this ministry as a modest form of reparation and penance for my previous obliviousness and complicity.

Furthermore, Fr. Bryan Massingale suggests that the BLM movement is consistent with fundamental Catholic beliefs of love, and that all lives are worthy of dignity. Yet why so much hostility towards it? He believes that BLM evokes white discomfort, distorts their innocence, and raises uncomfortable questions. He suggests that, unless there is the presence of transformational love within white souls, there can be little or no insight into systemic racism. Fr. Massingale goes on to say in his March 2021 presentation: "Anti-Blackness is a spiritual malady, a soul sickness, an interior malformation of a magnitude for which we lack words. It is an affliction that can only be healed when we learn how to love Blackness. Black Bodies. Black people. Only this kind of love — a radical love of, for, by, and with Black people — can make this old world a new world, a world where BLM, where Black Lives are sacred, where Black lives can breathe free."

176

Appendix

Glossary

- **Ad Hominem**: short for "argumentum ad hominem," refers to several types of arguments, some but not all of which are fallacious. Typically, this term refers to a rhetorical strategy where the speaker attacks the character, motive, or some other attribute of the person making an argument rather than attacking the substance of the argument itself.

- **Bias**: prejudice in favor of or against one thing, person, or group compared with another, usually in a way considered to be unfair. _Implicit Bias_ is any unconsciously held set of associations about a social group. Implicit biases can result in the attribution of particular qualities to all individuals from that group, also known as stereotyping. Implicit biases are the product of learned associations and social conditioning.

- **Blood Diamonds**: known as such primarily in Africa where they are mined using slave labor and then sold to directly finance terrorist activities across the globe. They are called "blood diamonds" because, figuratively, there is blood on the hands of anyone who deals in them.

- **Chattel Slavery**: the owning of human beings as property able to be bought, sold, given, and inherited. Slaves in this context have no personal freedom or recognized rights to decide the direction of their own lives.

- **Cultural Appropriation**: the adoption of an element or elements of one culture or identity by members of another culture or identity. This can be controversial when members of a dominant culture appropriate from disadvantaged minority cultures.

- **Encyclical**: a letter addressed by the pope to all the bishops of the Church intended for wide or general circulation.

- **Enwhitenment**: per the Urban Dictionary: "The furthering of one's own wokeness at the expense of actually knowing what the non-white communities around you like, need, want, or do."; "Having your own racist version of knowledge and insight"; "Knowing a lot about Caucasian people and/or their culture."

- **Exceptionalism**: a theory that a nation, region, or political system is exceptional and does not conform to the norm.
- **Just War Theory**: a doctrine used to ensure war is morally justifiable through a series of criteria, all of which must be met for a war to be considered just.
- **Native American Apology Resolution**: In December 2009 President Obama signed this resolution in which the United States recognizes there have been years of official depredations, ill-conceived policies, the breaking of covenants by the federal government regarding Indian tribes and apologizes to all native peoples for the many instances of violence, maltreatment, and neglect inflicted on native peoples by citizens of the United States.
- **POC**: abbreviation for People of Color; another related abbreviation is BIPOC, Black and Indigenous Persons of Color; it is used since the most oppressed are Blacks and Indigenous and therefore deserving of their own term.
- **Prejudice**: a preconceived opinion not based on reason or actual experience.
- **Prophet**: a person regarded as an inspired teacher or proclaimer of the will of God.
- **Racism**
  - o **Individual Racism** refers to an individual's racist assumptions, beliefs or behaviors and is "a form of racial discrimination that stems from conscious and unconscious, personal prejudice" (Henry and Tator, 2006, p. 329)
  - o **Institutional Racism** describes societal patterns and structures that impose oppressive or otherwise negative conditions on identifiable groups on the basis of race or ethnicity. Oppression may come from business, the government, the health care system, the schools, or the court, among other institutions. This phenomenon may also be referred to as societal racism, institutionalized racism, or cultural racism. (ThoughtCo, Tom Head)
  - o **Structural, Societal, Systemic Racism** is the formalization of a set of institutional, historical, cultural, and interpersonal practices within a society that more often than not puts one social or ethnic group in a better position to succeed and at the same time disadvantages other groups in a consistent and constant matter that disparities develop between the groups over

a period of time. Societal racism has also been called structural racism because society is structured in a way that excludes substantial numbers of people from minority backgrounds from taking part in social institutions. Societal racism is sometimes referred to as systemic racism as well. (Lawrence, Keith; Keleher, Terry (2004). "Chronic Disparity: Strong and Pervasive Evidence of Racial Inequalities" (PDF). Poverty Outcomes; James, Carl E. (8 February 1996). Perspectives on Racism and the Human Services Sector: A Case for Change (2nd Revised ed.). University of Toronto Press. p. 27; Yancey-Bragg, N'dea. "What is systemic racism? Here's what it means and how you can help dismantle it." USA Today)

o An **Antiracist** *is* one who supports an antiracist policy through their actions or expressing an antiracist idea. A **Racist** is one who is supporting a racist policy through their actions or inaction or expressing a racist idea. (Kendi — see Chapter 7)

• **Triumphalism**: the attitude or belief that a particular doctrine, religion, culture, or social system is superior to and should triumph over all others

• **White Fragility**: White people in North America live in a social environment that protects and insulates them from race-based stress. This insulated environment of racial protection builds white expectations for racial comfort while at the same time lowering the ability to tolerate racial stress, leading to what is referred to as White Fragility. This is a state in which even a minimum amount of racial stress becomes intolerable, triggering a range of defensive moves. These moves include the outward display of emotions such as anger, fear, and guilt, and behaviors such as argumentation, silence, and leaving the stress-inducing situation. These behaviors, in turn, function to reinstate white racial equilibrium. (DiAngelo)

Richard Rohr terms:
• **Liminality**: from the Latin word līmen, meaning "a threshold;" it is the quality of ambiguity or disorientation that occurs in the middle stage of a rite of passage, when participants no longer hold their pre-ritual status but have not yet begun the transition to the status they will hold when the rite is complete. During a rite's liminal stage, participants "stand at the threshold" between their previous

way of structuring their identity, time, or community, and a new way, which completing the rite establishes. (Turner, Victor (1974). "Liminal to liminoid in play, flow, and ritual: An essay in comparative symbology". Rice University Studies; Nordic Work with Traumatised Refugees: Do We Really Care, edited by Gwynyth Overland, Eugene Guribye, Birgit.)

- **Order, Disorder, Reorder Cycle (ODR)**
  - **Order***:* We begin with almost entirely tribal thinking, mirroring the individual journey, which starts with an egocentric need for "order" and "self." Only gradually do we move toward inclusive love.
  - **Disorder***:* We slowly recognize the invitation to a "face to face" love affair through the biblical dialogue of election, failure, sin, and grace, which matures the soul. This is where we need wisdom teachers to guide us through our "disorder."
  - **Reorder**: Among a symbolic few, there is a breakthrough to unitive consciousness (for example, figures like Abraham and Sarah, Moses, David, the Psalmists, many of the prophets, Job, Mary, Mary Magdalene, Jesus, and Paul). This is also what some call enlightenment or salvation.

Rights vs. Privileges
(see https://www.differencebetween.com/difference
-between-right-and-vs-privilege)

Rights and privileges are components of most constitutions in democracies around the world. People typically know the literal meanings of both these words but can confuse the two concepts as they want their privileges just like their rights. Rights are granted by the constitution to individuals while privileges are those that provide immunity, benefit, or exemption to certain people or groups. Problems begin when people think of privilege as their right as they equate the two rather than being grateful for being given privileges.

Rights are societal norms in the form of freedoms that are available to people by virtue of being citizens of a country or as members of a society. Rights are considered as fundamental and inalienable. All citizens of a country are granted certain rights under its constitution. In fact, it would be wrong to say that rights are granted as they are there to be taken or claimed by people and said to be fundamental in nature.

Many of the rights that are so dear to the hearts of people such as right to vote, work, move freely inside the country, choose a profession, profess a religion and the right to education have gradually evolved with the passage of time and enlightenment of people. Right to equality is a right that has taken centuries to be accepted and declared legal in many countries. This is one right that ensures that there can be no discrimination based on color of skin, gender, religion, language, ethnicity etc. Author's note: I would also add the right to health care.

Privileges are special benefits or permissions granted to an individual or a group based upon status, class, rank, title, or special talent. Thus, privilege is a special right not available to all members of the society but is rather restricted to a chosen few in the society. While some members of the society enjoy this right, others are excluded or denied these rights. Examples of privilege include:

- Being Male
- Being Heterosexual
- Being Cisgender
- Being a Couple
- Having Height
- Having Beauty
- Age related advantages
- Socioeconomic advantages
- Being Able-bodied
- Religion affiliation advantages
- Having a Passport
- Birthplace/Location Based/Geographical advantages
- Being a non-immigrant
- Access to Transportation
- Being White; specifically, white privilege is the societal privilege that benefits white people over non-white people in some societies, particularly if they are otherwise under the same social, political, or economic circumstances. With roots in European colonialism and imperialism, and the Atlantic slave trade, white privilege has developed in circumstances that have broadly sought to protect white

racial privileges, various national citizenships and other rights or special benefits.

Program Suggestions for Sacred Conversations (SC) on Race and Action, Submitted to Roc/ACTS

• The white participant base must be broadened to go well beyond the "usual suspects" of parish social justice committee members and others.

• Any program must ensure that there is participant commitment to action once the program is completed and laser focused on the pursuit of antiracism advocacy and policies.

• The program should be explicit on discovering ways to eliminate white supremacy through evoking discussion on the depths of supremacist history and utilize the tremendous SC storytelling techniques to personalize the impact of that history through the sharing of Black experiences and stories.

• There should be some required pre-reading before any program; e.g., Kendi's books --- 'Stamped from the Beginning' and 'How To Be An Antiracist;' perhaps provide a choice between the two to maximize discussions. An additional thought is that participants consider purchasing their own books or get a copy(s) from the library; it would provide an initial indicator of authentic commitment.

• Coalitions and collaborative programming with other like-minded faith communities, organizations, etc., are preferable vs. acting independently and therefore sustaining Rochester's inclination to be a 'silo' factory.

• I fully endorse Pastor Wanda Wilson's suggestion about the necessity of having more Black facilitators but I urge caution on letting that pursuit distract and delay the urgent need for white engagement. Why couldn't a program be developed for whites to orient, learn, guide, etc., *themselves* regarding the history of White Supremacy? Then after they went through this initial "whites only" program, Part II could be what is now titled 'Sacred Conversations on Race and Action' but revamped and updated based on the white supremacist events of 2020-2021.

• Said another way, offer a variety of approaches for individuals, faith communities, etc., to consider ... but don't let the requirement for Black facilitators (trainers for whites!?) interfere with the essential need for whites to do their own individual work in combating racism, especially males

• Lastly, Roc/ACTS (R/A) is VERY White and VERY Catholic and it speaks volumes on several levels. The true depths of white Catholic leadership engagement, however, should be explored and there should be more active promotion of R/A and its antiracism initiatives. Another recommendation is periodic (at least monthly) antiracism sermons from the pulpit by respective parish pastors premised on the USCCB's 2018 letter on racism. This would serve to provide more frequency of important antiracism messaging to the people in the pews (or in their homes via Zoom) that can't be done simply via parish bulletins, information on websites, etc.

Discussions with the Fairport Central School District and Fairport Town Board in Late 2019 and Early 2020

The Fairport superintendent and the board president told me in late 2019 the FCSD had historically done a great job with special needs students and was continuing in that tradition, they did not believe that the D&C articles were accurate and that the reporter's data was flawed, referenced 2-3 FCSD programs that addressed equity and diversity, and indicated they were about to launch a community-based diversity council.

I submitted a Freedom of Information Act request to the FCSD regarding student transfers between 2016 and 2018. I found that there were 62 movements of Fairport minority students into Rochester involving 35 families over the three academic years.

With approximately 5,000 students, at least 95 percent white, with and at best about 250 non-white in the Fairport district, the minority movements, especially those that were Black, are statistically significant.

I received vague reasons for the movements, so at a subsequent board meeting I suggested that if the FCSD story line is so positive, then the district should go public and refute the D&C articles, make this issue a formal agenda item at a future board meeting, and that the superintendent meet with me and others who have reached out to the board to discuss this matter as a group that would include the two Monroe County legislators from Fairport.

I received no feedback on these suggestions.

In the months afterward, I had several discussions with one supportive FCSD Board member (who is now the board president), submitted comments to the January 2020 board meeting, wrote letters to two county legislators, invited members of the three governmental boards to attend the upcoming SC program, contacted the D&C executive editor and was told that the reporter who wrote the article had been on leave and would get back to me, attended two sessions of FCSD's Equity & Diversity program (Lead by Example), designed to elicit challenging conversations among parents and interested community members, participated in a focus group session in connection with the FCSD's Equity & Diversity Audit, and resubmitted a request for FCSD's transfer policies.

This activity led to discussions with a board member and the superintendent as well as one response from a county legislator; at least four other Fairport residents wrote their own letters, attended board meetings, etc.; kept many in the COTA-COR community informed; and an FCSD Board person on its policy committee promised a full review of transfer policies and would follow up with me.

I have continued the discussion with the Fairport Village and Town boards.

Program participants at the SC session on March 14, 2020, made recommendations to:

- Utilize our white privilege to foster effective antiracism actions, behavior, and policies i.e., root out white supremacy.
- Advocate for the city, county, and state to address the housing crisis and support construction of affordable housing below 50 percent of Area Median Income (AMI).
- Advocate for antiracist zoning policy with your town and village boards.
- Petition and work with the county to research and develop a different methodology of allocating property tax revenues to equalize housing and learning opportunities between the city and towns.
- Contact other suburban school districts about possible "dumping."
- Continue to pressure the Chamber and its new "ROC2025" ini-

tiative for specific connection with the RCSD, especially mentoring, training, and workforce development. Also, engagement with the TID Coalition and the city's REAL initiative.

- Support the City Roots Community Land Trust.
- Fight income discrimination in your town.
- Support the city-wide Tenant Union and the Rochester Homeless Union.
- Ask your school board to teach more comprehensive history on the total American experience.
- Focus and consider how best to create a powerful coalition(s) among us that lead to movement(s) for needed change on consequential institutional racism issues.
- Provide more Sacred Conversations programming.
- Present an antiracism presence on parish website.
- Promote a parish antiracism program model in the diocese and other parishes.
- Respond to letters from incarcerated persons; provide direction on how they can help themselves.
- Patronize Black and other minority owned businesses.
- Build relationships via one-to-one conversations with POC and with your own race.
- Other advocacy via letters, research, e.g., humane alternative to solitary confinement; bail reform; voting rights; politicians to be contacted.
- Engage with the upcoming Civil Rights Park in the city.
- Provide input on the Perinton and Fairport ten-year master plan update processes.

Why we capitalized Black, not white

It wasn't long ago that the major publishing style guides preferred using the terms "black" and "white" to describe groups of people in lower-case. That has changed in the past few years. The Associated Press, which has 1,400 member newspapers and broadcasters, revised its style in July 2020 to capitalize Black in a racial, ethnic or cultural sense, "conveying a shared sense of history, identity and community among people who identify as Black, including those in the African diaspora and within Africa."

AP style continues to not capitalize white as a reference to a group of people as "after a review and period of consultation, we found, at this time, less support for capitalizing white. White people generally do not share the same history and culture, or the experience of being discriminated against because of skin color. In addition, AP is a global news organization and there is considerable disagreement, ambiguity and confusion about whom the term includes in much of the world."

The *Chicago Manual of Style*, the guidelines of which are adhered to by many book publishers, changed its stance on this style in June 2020 to follow AP style, preferring to capitalize Black and not white, albeit with the following caveat: "We continue to recognize that individual preferences will vary, and we acknowledge that usage may depend on context."

Beyond the AP and Chicago guides, other publishing entities or style guides such as *Columbia Journalism Review, The Diversity Style Guide* and others, agreed on capitalizing Black. "These decisions align with long-standing capitalization of distinct racial and ethnic identifiers such as Latino, Asian American and Native American," the AP said in announcing its decision.

With these major style guides either mandating or perferring to capitalize Black and lower-case white, we felt that unless we had an overwhelmingly compelling argument to go against these guides, we'd follow them. After studying the reason behind the decisions made by several of these guides, we could not find such an overwhelmingly compelling argument.

Bibliography

Alexander, Michelle. *The New Jim Crow: Mass Incarceration in the Age of Colorblindness*. New York: [Jackson, Tenn.]: New Press; Distributed by Perseus Distribution, 2010.

Anderson, Carol. *White Rage*. London: Bloomsbury Publishing, 2016

Baldwin, James. *The Fire Next Time*. New York: Dial Press, 1963

Bennett, Britt. *The Vanishing Half*. New York: Riverhead Books 2020

Berry, Wendell. *The Hidden Wound*. Berkeley, California: Counterpoint Press, 2010

Bovy, Phoebe Maltz. *The Perils of Privilege*. New York: St. Martin's Press, 2017

Boyle, Gregory. *Tattoos on The Heart*. New York: Free Press, 2009.

Charles, Mark and Soong-Chan, Rah. *Unsettling Truths*. Westmont, Illinois: InterVarsity Press, 2019

Coates, Ta-Nehisi. *Between the World and Me*. New York: Spiegel & Grau, 2015

Coates, Ta-Nehisi. *Case for Reparations*. The Atlantic, June 2014 issue

Coates, Ta-Nehisi. *We Were Eight Years in Power*. New York: Penguin Random House, 2018

Collins, Chuck. *Born on Third Base*. Hartford, Vermont: Chelsea Green Publishing, 2016

Cone, James H. *The Cross and the Lynching Tree*. Maryknoll, NY: Orbis Books, 2013.

Cummins, Jeanine. *American Dirt*. New York: Flatiron Books, 2020

Desmond, Matthew. *Evicted*. New York: Crown, 2016

DiAngelo, Robin. *Nice Racism*. Boston: Beacon Press, 2021

DiAngelo, Robin. *White Fragility*. Boston: Beacon Press, 2018

Dyson, Michael Eric. *Tears We Cannot Stop*. New York: St. Martin's Press, 2017

Eberhardt, Jennifer Lynn. Biased. New York: Penguin, 2019

Fr. Richard Rohr, OFM books, writings, daily meditations; see www.cac.org

Glaude, Eddie S. Jr. *Begin Again*. New York: Penguin Random House, 2021

Grainger, Jean. *The Emerald Horizon*. Independently published: 2019

Grainger, Jean. *The Star and the Shamrock*. Independently published: 2019

Holmes, Barbara. *Crisis Contemplation*. Center for Action & Contemplation, 2021

Irving, Debby. *Waking Up White*. Elephant Room Press, 2014

Johnston, David Cay. *Divided*. New York: The New Press, 2015.

Jones, Van. *Beyond the Messy Truth*. New York: Random House, 2017

Kendi, Ibram X. *Stamped From the Beginning: The Definitive History of Racist Ideas in America.* New York: Nation Books, 2017.

Kendi, Ibram. *How to Be an Antiracist.* London, England: Bodley Head, 2019.

Lee, Harper. *To Kill a Mockingbird,* Philadelphia: J. B. Lippincott & Co., 1960

Levitsky, Steven; Ziblatt, Daniel. *How Democracies Die.* New York: Penguin Random House, 2018

Mann, Charles C. *1491.* New York: Knopf, 2005

McGhee, Heather. *The Sum of Us,.* New York: One World, 2021

Meacham, Jon. *His Truth Is Marching On.* New York: Random House, 2020

Metzl, Jonathan M. *Dying of Whiteness.* New York: Basic Books, 2019

Mich, Marvin L. Krier. *The Challenge and Spirituality of Catholic Social Teaching.* New York: Orbis Books, 2011

Moskowitz, P.E. *How to Kill a City.* Public Affairs, 2017

Nerburn, Kent. *Neither Wolf nor Dog.* New World Library, 1994

Ng, Celeste. *Everything I Never Told You.* New York: Penguin, 2014

Ng, Celeste. *Little Fires Everywhere.* New York: Penguin, 2017

Perlman, Elliot. *The Street Sweeper.* New York: Riverhead Books, 2012.

Pope Francis, *Fratelli Tutti.* Vatican Press, 2020

Rah, Soong Chan. *Prophetic Lament.* Downer's Grove, Illinois: InterVarsity Press, 2015

Rothstein, Richard. *The Color of Law.* New York: Liveright, 2018

Soboroff, Jacob. *Separated.* New York: HarperCollins, 2020

Stallworth, Ron. *BlackKKlansman.* New York: Flatiron Books, 2014

Stevenson, Bryan. Just Mercy: A Story of Justice and Redemption. New York: Spiegel & Grau, 2014.

Strazzabosco, John. *Ninety Feet Under.* Burlington, Ontario, Canada: Word & Deed Publishing Incorporated, 2018

Taibbi, Matt. *I Can't Breathe.* New York: Spiegel & Grau, 2017

Treuer, David. *Heartbeat from Wounded Knee.* New York: Penguin, 2019

Vance, J.D. *Hillbilly Elegy.* New York: Harper, 2016

Walliss, Jim. *America's Original Sin.* Ada, Michigan: Baker Publishing Group, 2015

Ward, Jesmyn. *The Fire This Time.* New York: Simon & Schuster, 2016

Whitehead, Colson. *The Nickel Boys.* New York: Doubleday, 2019

Whitehead, Colson. *Underground Railroad.* New York: Doubleday, 2016

Wilkerson, Isabel. *Caste: The Origins of our Discontents.* New York: Random House, 2020

Wilkerson, Isabel. *The Warmth of Other Suns: the Epic Story of America's Great Migration.* New York: Vintage Books, 2011.

https://www.persuasion.community/p/the-painful-path-to-unity?token=ey-J1c2VyX2lkIjoxNDkxODI3OCwicG9zdF9pZCI6MzUxMTI5ODcsIl8iOi-JRK0xoZSIsImlhdCI6MTYxOTTAxMjU5MiwiZXhwIjoxNjE5MDE2MT-kyLCJpc3MiOiJwdWItNjE1NzkkLCJzdWIiOiJwb3N0LXJlYWN0aW9uIn0.pYanzmX4QzJ2q13AxtJCksP_z_OCcodSwZusunlYzSw

W.E. WYNNE

Article Re: Guns and Race:
https://heathercoxrichardson.substack.com/p/april-19-2021?token=ey-J1c2VyX2lkIjozMDIwMjQwMiwicG9zdF9pZCI6MzUzNjQ5MDEsIl8iOi-JvR2xlaSIsImlhdCI6MTYxOTU1NjYwNSwiZXhwIjoxNjE5NTYwMjA1LC-Jpc3MiOiJwdWItMjA1MzMiLCJzdWIiOiJwb3N0LXJlYWN0aW9uIn0.
OJbs_ZovjZSTPqRNWReoni_TwOGzGyfj0KZffrBzy7I&utm_source=sub-stack&utm_medium=email&utm_content=share

About the Author

Bill Wynne is retired and a white antiracist activist in the Rochester, New York, area. A first-time author of Understanding and *Combating* Racism: My Path from Oblivious American to Evolving Activist, the foundation of Wynne's experiential insights in this memoir is premised on the human networks and friendships he developed in his business career and then his subsequent work in the nonprofit sector for many years. This was further complemented through extensive decades-long engagement and leadership roles with many church and community organizations. Bill's social and racial justice activism is a lived example demonstrating the importance and power of diverse and meaningful relationships which is one of the key through lines of his memoir.

Raised Catholic by second generation German and Irish parents and the oldest of six siblings, Bill had a full array of Catholic education from the Sisters of St. Joseph in elementary school, to the Jesuits in high school, and then the Franciscans in college. He eventually received his MBA at the more secular University of Rochester during his over thirty-year career in telecommunications.

Before moving on to the nonprofit sector for ten years, he walked the 500-mile-long pilgrimage in northern Spain known as the Camino de Santiago. The physical, mental, and spiritual challenges he faced during this month-long trek were complicated by the timing ... departing ten days after "9/11" and returning shortly after the bombing of Afghanistan, the beginning of a twenty-year war.

After retiring in 2014, Bill immediately began searching for ways to be more "hands-on' with social and racial justice activism as well as to broaden his knowledge about racism. He read countless books and led book reviews, attended scores of programs and conferences, and got educated on the disturbing racial history of this country that was not taught when he was growing up.

The timing could not have been better given the tragic Mr. Michael Brown police killing in St. Louis that year, then the political transition from a Black to white President, the many resulting tragic impacts during that shift from the incident in Charlottesville, to the Mr. George Floyd murder, and the Capitol insurrection to name just three. With his knowledge deepened, Bill got more active by developing several racism awareness programs and antiracism advocacy.

Eventually by mid-2020, the "call" for Bill to tell his story came at him in several ways and he was led to tell the story of how he came to understand the impact of whiteness through his life and his personal obliviousness.

Serving as essential guides on his most current pilgrimage were several Black friends most of whom Bill had just met over the past seven years. Some thought his voice needed to be heard through the lens of a white Catholic male who went from virtually complete unknowingness about the depths of racism (just like most whites) to become an informed and participative antiracism advocate. One white friend in his Fr. Richard Rohr discussion group calls Bill a "contemplative activist."

Bill's most important support, however, emanates from the love and support of his wife of almost fifty years, Sandy, and their three children and four grandchildren. Similar to the Camino but much more demanding, he could not have written this book without them "walking" in solidarity on this challenging and ever-changing road to understanding and moving towards a full antiracism commitment. A living example of his family's participation was through the establishment in 2018 of the 'Wynne-Strauss Fund for Social and Racial Justice' through the Rochester Community Foundation. The process has been established for grants from this fund to be made for virtually the rest of this century and to assist with this, all proceeds from the sale of this memoir will be directed to the fund.

Please consider joining him on this essential antiracism movement for our country, the world, and most importantly our children and grandchildren. Bill can be reached at the website www.wewynneauthor.com or via email at william wynneauthor@gmail.com.

"70 x 7"

Visit us at
www.PathBinderPublishing.com

This title is also available as an e-book

Made in United States
North Haven, CT
25 May 2023

36958050R00107